CHAMPIONSHIP

SELLING

CHAMPIONSHIP SELLING

A BLUEPRINT FOR WINNING WITH TODAY'S CUSTOMER

TOM BLAKE

TOM HODSON

TONY ENRICO

John Wiley & Sons Canada, Ltd.

Library and Archives Canada Cataloguing in Publication Data

Blake, Tom, 1951–
     Championship selling : a blueprint for winning with today's customer / Tom Blake, Tom Hodson, Tony Enrico.

Includes index.
ISBN-13 978-0-470-83675-0
ISBN-10 0-470-83675-X

1. Selling. I. Hodson, Tom, 1958– II. Enrico, Tony, 1965– III. Title.

HF5438.25.B53 2005   658.85   C2005-903689-3

Production Credits:

Cover and interior text design: Natalia Burobina

Printer: Tri-Graphic Printing Ltd.

John Wiley & Sons Canada, Ltd.
6045 Freemont Blvd.
Mississauga, Ontario
L5R 4J3

Printed in Canada

10 9 8 7 6 5 4 3 2 1

Dedications

For my mother, Theresa, and sister, Lynda, who gave me the chance to be where I am today; my wife and best friend, Suzanne, who continually makes a difference in people's lives and gives me a vision of what is possible; my wonderful children and grandchildren, Marty and Theresa, Sara, Jani, Martha, Ethan and McKenzie, who have taught me so much about life; and all of the Blake and McLuckie families—I love you very much.

— Tom Blake

To the dream team: my wife, Joanne, you are an extraordinary gift, thank you for giving me happiness, and my children, Caitrin, Sean, Lauren and Cristin, you are the loves of my life; my mom and dad, Beverly and Ray, you are my mentors and role models; my brothers, Doug, Scott and Ken, and my sister, Megan, for who you all are and have become; my mother-in-law, Terry, brothers-in-law, Neil, Kevin, Gerald, David and Marvin, and sisters-in-law, Michelle, Kim, Lisa, Elaine, Karen, Jane, Susan and Paola, for adding your own flair to the Hodson clan; my late father-in-law, Tom O'Connor—Tom, I think you would have liked this; and my late Nana, who loved all things literary.

— Tom Hodson

To my wife, Michelle, whose boundless love, kindness and friendship have helped me create a remarkable life; my children, Nick and Alec, whose depth and reason astound me at every turn and who bring constant joy to our family; and my mom, dad and brothers, for being such beautiful parts of my life— there is no such thing as coincidence.

— Tony Enrico

Table of Contents

PART TWO

The Performance Pyramid

Acknowledgements

The expertise, encouragement and insights of a great many people helped us see this book through to completion. Thanks first and foremost to I.J. Schecter for transforming our raw thoughts into graceful prose—your help and direction spurred us toward the finish line and through the tape. Thanks to all the incredible customers and extraordinary individuals we have been fortunate to serve over the past decade, including, with specific regard to this book, Steve Bigford at Quaker Tropicana Gatorade, Steve Fox at Nestlé, David House at American Express, Tim Hedges of McCain foods, Ray Lamont of Lamont Insurance, Julie Lange at ScotiaMcLeod, Tom Muccio, formerly of Procter & Gamble, Joe Pal of Pal Financial and Blair Ruelens at Cadbury Adams. Thanks to those who took the time to speak with us and expand our own perspectives, like Richard Touzalin and Thomas Szaky. Thanks to Grant McClement, a former cog in the Optimé wheel and one of the sharpest customer business development thinkers anywhere; thanks to Don Jones and the entire exper!ence it team for partnering with us to conceive truly groundbreaking work; thanks to Paul Davidson at Open Text

Corporation and James Blackburn of A. James Fifth & Company for providing us rich story material; thanks to our other business partners at Employer Consultancy INC, Data Sense and ENS for helping us to learn, stretch and grow every day. And thanks especially to the Optimé International team—Cheryl Cameron, Marti Cleveland-Innes, Audri Els, Deb Voigt-Hetland, Hugues Gibeault, Bonnie Niedojadlo, Elyse Richard, Carolyn Taves, Peter Townsend and Valerie Walls—for whose wisdom, support and tireless contribution we are inexpressibly thankful. It may be our names on the cover, but yours belong there, too.

Finally, we extend our highest appreciation and deepest love to our wonderful families, who support us unconditionally in our daily lives and who, during the course of writing this book, assured us repeatedly that we really did have something to say.

You are champions all.

Introduction

Selling is everyone's business. We're all affected by it, every day of our lives. Look around the room or office where you're reading these words. Everything you see—from the chair you're sitting on to the computer on your desk—has been bought and sold, and each of the items filling your space satisfies a different, specific need.

Though most people intuitively understand the value of buying and selling, few companies are moving from understanding to actually doing something about it. Those moving in a winning direction, having cut costs and streamlined operations to every extent, are realizing that the opposite effort—business building and customer acquisition—carries greater value in the long term.

As a result, the sales function is beginning to take its overdue place at the forefront of successful business practice, and the customer development skills that define it are growing more and more valuable. Where salespeople may once have been lone wolves, today they are multifunctional customer managers versed in business fundamentals and operational strategies. Where in the past it may have been common for organizations to pace along myopically focused on their own bottom lines, today it is those with a resolute championship mentality and strict outward focus who come out on top.

At every level of industry, companies able to interact effectively with customers are separating themselves from the pack. With this shift comes tremendous opportunity at both the individual and organizational levels. Sales ambassadors adopting a true customer focus have before them an unlimited ceiling of possibility. Organizations dedicating themselves to a customer orientation are poised to create enormous value. And the combination of these two forces, harnessed thoughtfully, can generate unprecedented levels of performance.

This book is written for both the aspiring sales champion and the business leader committed to guiding his or her company forward through the fiercely competitive waters of twenty-first-century business. In our dual experience as practitioners (we have spent significant portions of our careers as sales professionals) and coaches (we work with Fortune 500 companies to turbocharge their sales organizations) we understand, from the inside out, the extraordinary potential that lies, waiting to be unleashed, within the sales function. We begin by reviewing, at a macro level, the factors that have combined to place selling at the very core of business today. From there we take a journey up the Performance Pyramid, a framework of concepts and processes intended to move you beyond simple understanding and into championship execution.

Ultimately, this execution involves something far greater than business success. In all of our numerous interviews for this book, we asked the following question: *At the end of the day, what is selling all about?* We were amazed at the frequency of a particular answer, one that captures the essence of what it means to be a championship sales professional: *It's about making a difference in people's lives.*

We believe passionately in this idea, and we hope the concepts and principles in *Championship Selling* will help you become the kind of champion who makes a difference in your customers' lives every day.

Tom Blake
Tom Hodson
Tony Enrico

PART ONE

The Sales Revolution

CHAPTER 1

Embracing the Shift

You can make more friends in two months by becoming really interested in other people than you can in two years by trying to get other people interested in you.
—Dale Carnegie

A fundamental shift is occurring in business. Customers are shrewder and more sophisticated than ever before. They can no longer be manipulated to fit a product a company is selling. Today, the product must fit the customer.

The vision for the new world of business development will see entire companies focusing their resources on helping customers deliver on their agendas. Companies that revolutionize their approach to customer development will win, and individuals throughout these winning organizations will not only talk the mantra of customer-centricity but also live it.

There is a particular barometer we like to use to gauge where companies fall on the customer-centricity scale. It's called the Customer Challenge—though it isn't for customers.

Choose a sampling of individuals across your company, in various functions and at various levels, and ask them three questions:

- Who are our top ten customers?

- How much business do we do with each of them?

- What are their goals and priorities for the next twelve to twenty-four months, and how are we helping deliver against these?

In a customer-centric sales organization—what we call a championship selling culture—the answers to these questions come readily. In most organizations, however, such answers are not forthcoming. Up and down the organizational ladder and across divisions, people are able to speak at length and in detail about what is going on inside the company. However, when asked about the situation on the outside—with customers—they falter.

To help these people stake out a more customer-oriented path, we often recommend a simple but powerful first step: create a cue card, to be carried at all times, listing the answers to the questions above. Most important, what are their customers trying to achieve, and how are they helping the customers do it?

We're frequently amazed at how powerful a guide this little cue card becomes. It helps people shape their discussions with peers, subordinates and superiors. It enables them to brainstorm solutions more creatively. It allows them to structure their thinking in a more strategic way. And it serves as a constant reminder of where a championship salesperson and a championship organization need to be focused.

But let's take a step back.

Entrenched in every culture throughout the world, at every stage of the human record, is a powerful instinct for mutual advancement through the simple process of give and take. Rewind the clock six thousand years, for example, and we discover sun-baked merchants hauling grains and fabrics to be sold at a market in Cairo. Jump ahead a few millennia and we encounter a great Egyptian queen solidifying her standing via a trade voyage down the Nile into the African interior. Looking in on medieval Europe, we observe hundreds of agricultural laborers starting to call themselves smiths, tailors, coopers and wheelwrights and opening small shops in the village to promote their services or wares. Stride forward again and we see Jacques Cartier seeking a passage to Asia, instead landing on the shore of the Gaspé Peninsula, then trading with the Indians who paddle out to greet him and unknowingly lighting the first spark in a thriving industry that will fuel the exploration of half a continent.

These scenes, and countless others throughout history, provide glimpses into a broad kaleidoscope of people and groups pursuing the creation of value through selling. Each character in this long-running drama helps show that, even in our earliest forms, we were attempting to master the rules of exchange, attempting to create moments where those on both sides of the swap came away feeling a reciprocal good had been achieved.

Frozen in time like squares on a quilt, these scenes illustrate the fabric that has woven together our social tapestry since the beginning of civilization: the evolution of exchange, the process of buying and selling, the course of giving to get. In different ways and according to different norms, we have always bought and sold. Currencies may change from spices to furs to gold to paper money. Such occurrences are merely the shifting commodities behind which a fundamental process remains.

No matter how big—or small—the world of business becomes, the engine ultimately driving commerce can still be boiled down to individual interactions, vendor to consumer, seller to buyer, person to person. Though the inner workings of today's organizations are becoming increasingly vast as more and more companies vertically integrate, divest, merge and expand, no deal is completed, no sale made, no contract signed—no value generated—without the successful interface of two parties, one selling, one buying.

Today, selling remains at the root of successful business. From multinational powerhouses to fast-growing organizations to world-beating entrepreneurs, those companies making the biggest leaps in the twenty-first century owe their status not to luck or accidental timing but to a combination of careful study of their customers and well-considered delivery of their products or services.

Those who operate on the front line for these organizations, those who not only make plans but also execute customer interactions, are the individuals who drive this change. They are indispensable agents of the transmission of knowledge and capability that allows their companies to move forward. As business continues to evolve and customers become increasingly sophisticated, selling skills become powerful instruments of success. And those who possess such skills become more influential driving forces of this success than ever before.

A Little Attention Goes a Long Way

Recently we spoke with a senior vice president at a leading global food company that had recently merged with another. The SVP had been surprised to learn that both companies involved were significantly underdeveloped with a particular customer. This customer hadn't been assigned a dedicated account executive, since the customer wasn't considered big enough to warrant undue attention or resources.

The SVP, believing every high-potential customer required focused attention and resources, assigned an account executive. He told this account executive he wanted two things: first, to get the company to embrace this customer and think externally; second, to double the business—to 100,000 cases—within two years. He would provide support, but he wanted the account executive to lead.

The account executive seized the reins, quickly engaging the entire company by requesting that members within each organizational function meet with the customer to better understand its objectives. This seemingly obvious step led to powerful results, including the company being named Vendor of the Year by the customer.

More important, thanks to the account executive's efforts to align the company with the customer's goals, the SVP's business objective was missed by a significant amount. The company didn't end up selling 100,000 cases; it sold 1.5 million.

THE SALES FUNCTION: MOVING TO THE FORE

Some companies derive tremendous benefit from integrating customer business development as an organization-wide process.

Others are playing catch-up. Over time, the value of selling has, in a variety of ways, been ignored or misunderstood. Now some companies are beginning to align themselves closely around the sales function, but many still treat it as a separate entity rather than a company-wide process upon which success turns.

Companies are beginning to realize that employees directly engaged in customer interaction are worth their weight in gold. There is a new phase of business evolution: the ability to sell—to drive new business, to maintain customer focus as an ongoing strategy rather than just the trend of the month. Selling is finding its way to the head of business priority, and those companies paying heed to the customer imperative are seeing the results.

As organizations struggle to hit upon the magic formula that will vault them past competitors into new levels of sustainable advantage, they are discovering a solution so obvious it has been passed over time and again. The basic touchpoint around which they must weave themselves today is the same one that has driven business success since the first businesses came into being: selling.

Selling was once considered a part of a process that occurred naturally, on the periphery of a company's operations. Leading organizations today know better, and they are dedicating greater time, energy and financial resources to the sales function and to those who sell.

They realize that everyone is selling every day, including people within their organizations. Logistics is constantly selling to Finance, Finance sells to HR, HR sells to IT and IT sells to Operations. They are asking themselves tough questions: How often does sales factor into business strategy and not merely business execution? They recognize that selling is a cross-functional process that needs to be developed from the inside so benefits can be seen on the outside.

This opportunity extends from the corporate world to the academic. Throughout the twentieth century, business schools invested relatively meager amounts of time and energy in developing curriculums specifically tailored to the selling function in business. Most schools focused on concepts such as finance, brand marketing and operations. Recently academia has begun to pay some attention to the value of sales, though primarily as a branch of a traditional curriculum rather than a function with its own needs and particularities. If business schools increase the focus on selling as the fastest-growing mechanism of business success today, they will have the opportunity to create championship salespeople and drivers of meaningful organization change.

CHAPTER 2

Making the Connection

Motivate them, train them, care about them, and make winners out of them...they'll treat the customers right. And if customers are treated right, they'll come back.
—J. Willard Marriott Jr.

Like a circuit board with a single wire left unattached, many organizations have plenty of power channeled directly into the company effort but require one more critical connection. Today's leaders can maximize the incredible potential in that one dormant wire by committing to plugging it in.

Companies that have acknowledged the sales function and customer business development as core competencies are carrying the torch of success in today's corporate battlefield. Farsighted corporate leaders recognize that selling is not only a vibrant process characterized by subtlety and skill, but also the most direct link to the customer. Properly managed, this link can make a serious difference to business. Clearly, leaders of every type are beginning to think more about the importance of customer interaction.

In the current corporate environment of media training and carefully prepared sound bytes, talking the talk is common. But leaders dedicated to business building are doing more, by acting on—not just talking about—the value of customer interface. These individuals have committed themselves and their companies to driving championship agendas. They have established powerful new links by consistently growing and expanding their sales talent through innovative stretch assignments, training and peer development activities.

In addition to plugging sales into the upper strata of their organizations, today's customer-oriented leaders create a sales-positive environment by getting to know those on their front line. They enhance their knowledge of the customer by enhancing their knowledge of their own salespeople. The top customer-centric leaders focus not on a superficial interface with the sales organization, but on genuinely working to further the company's business-building opportunities by helping their salespeople excel individually and collectively.

Such leaders take the old perception—that sales is an entity outside the organization—and reverse it. They communicate the clear message that those who execute the selling function represent the company's very lifeblood. Take, for example, Jeffrey R. Immelt, CEO and Chair of the Board for General Electric. In his letter to stakeholders as part of GE's 2004 annual report, Immelt says:

> *CEOs cannot delegate growth or customer satisfaction.*
> *I try to spend at least five days each month with*

customers or being otherwise involved in the selling process. I get involved with important new growth activities. And twice each month I do town hall meetings with several hundred customers to share ideas on the direction of GE and listen to their thoughts on what we can do better.

A good number of today's managers and executives who think they have a customer-centric outlook fail to practice or instill customer-centric action. Many senior executives insist they do all the things a championship person ought to, but in fact they demonstrate that the leap to a championship approach, though simple in theory, is hindered by our natural instinct to look at things based on our own needs.

Senior leaders manage many important decisions every day. Yet the more points of misalignment between a company, its salespeople and its customers, the higher the probability that numbers will suffer. When the misalignment becomes too great, it can permanently disrupt everything the company is trying to achieve. However, when a company is fully aligned to its customer's situation, the relationship between the two is like the teeth of a zipper, neatly connected from top to bottom. Senior leaders who come to understand this will inspire a company-wide migration to customer-centric thinking and ultimately witness the results in both the top and bottom lines.

The shift is not necessarily an easy one. Today's senior executive is a frenetic creature, often overseeing teams located on different continents, flying thousands of miles for meetings that last only a few hours, balancing concrete business problems with sensitive interpersonal dynamics and dealing with adamant instructions from parent bodies to streamline operations.

It is this last aspect the executive must not interpret as a need to cut costs. On the contrary: when sales is plugged into an organization at its core, the instinct to cut costs is replaced with the organization-wide effort to create true customer value. The organization's leaders stop focusing on internal assessments to see where salaries can be removed, operating costs lowered or expenses reduced. Instead, they leverage true business-building skills to deliver value to the customer. In the past, leadership mentality was to slash costs first and ask questions later. Executives believed boards and company shareholders would see such moves as prudent. In today's business culture, it is the ability to harness the talent of the sales organization to deliver creative and innovative solutions that distinguishes the top leaders from those still seeking areas in which to pare.

In shifting their focus from the bottom line to the top line—where the customer exists—today's leaders can take their organizations to new levels. This change will result not from stripping operations but from learning how to serve customers' needs through the creation of mutually beneficial business-building solutions. Companies will become more streamlined when they waste less time and money trying to figure out how to fulfill their own desires and instead learn about, and meet, the desires of the customer.

A 2004 study by IBM Business Consulting Services, *Consumer Products 2010: Executing to Lead in a World of Extremes*, reveals that a majority of top executives are beginning to focus more on revenue growth than on cost reduction. "Our company, like most players in our sector," said one executive, "is beyond the cost-cutting stage. Now it is about growing the top line while keeping the bottom line in check."

THE ASPIRING SALES CHAMPION

In many companies, salespeople spend more time trying to influence their own organizations than they do selling to their customers. These companies invest significant time and energy making sure other parts of the organization are well armed to do their jobs at the highest level. The finance team is assigned auditors to verify the integrity of its work; the marketing team is told to hire an agency to render the brand vision in an inventive way; the IT department is connected 24/7 with support centers in far-flung destinations. The sales organization, however—the only group visibly representing the company to customers—is asked to be self-sufficient or to operate with limited resources. In other words, people in sales are left the unenviable job of trying to force the customer to align with their organization instead of working to align the two enterprises. This method of doing business is called transactional selling (described by Neil Rackham in *Spin Selling*), and the salespeople within transactional organizations are trapped by their companies' inward focus.

One doesn't require a degree in psychology to know that people react aversively when they feel they're being shoehorned into someone else's agenda. As long as a transactional mentality continues to exert pressure, senior leaders continue to spend resources to determine what aspect of the company's products or services is failing to lure customers.

Today, the transactional trend is changing. More and more companies are shifting their attention toward the customer. As these companies move past transactional selling—the essence of which is to close and move on, with little attention paid to the customer—to championship selling—the objective of which is complete alignment with the customer—people in sales grow in value. Suddenly, the drive and ambition of those on the customer front line are the most important assets within the organization. The opportunity for aspiring championship salespeople has arrived. In a world where the customer reigns supreme, the person who knows the customer best brings the greatest worth.

The company that recognizes this truth rises above the pack by nurturing the ambition of its salespeople and cultivating their championship skills. Organizations that continue to align themselves inward, rather than around the customer, continue to tie the hands of their salespeople. Organizations that continue to align themselves outward by investing in their salespeople will become more versed in how their products fit—or don't fit—the customer's specific needs. They will grow their bottom lines by paying attention to their top lines.

Could I Get Some Training Here?

A large opportunity to satisfy the drive of aspiring sales champions lies in formal training programs. Providing salespeople the proper tools to fulfill customer agendas requires a commitment to closing the gap between organization and customer. No more are salespeople governed by a survival-of-the-fittest hierarchy. In championship organizations, those in the sales organization are no longer handed a product or service to sell, told a few superficial things about it, furnished with an impressively thick instruction booklet, taken through a lavish marketing meeting and sent into the field with a word of encouragement and a reminder about the incentive gifts awarded to the top sellers at the end of the month. They are trained in championship principles (which we will discuss in Part Two), supported by other functions, and, as a result, leave transactional competitors scratching their heads.

Today's leading companies have performed a necessary one-eighty, shifting significant resources toward acquiring, and satisfying, customers through the efforts of their salespeople. Indeed, some companies are training their salespeople in core customer-facing skills. These companies are training their salespeople to go out into the field, find the *customer's* agenda, then bring it back to the organization.

A 2003 study by Accenture entitled *Changing Sales Force Behavior to Achieve High Performance* reveals that, despite expressing dissatisfaction with the performance of their salespeople, many company leaders make no additional investment in them. The authors of the study offer two specific ways companies can dramatically improve sales organization performance: first, by spelling out more explicitly the link between salespeople's behaviors and the objectives of the company, and second, by implementing new human resource and training programs to strengthen salespeople's abilities as well as the context in which work is performed.

Executives express an almost universal conviction regarding the importance of sales and customer interaction. In the Accenture study, nearly two hundred corporate executives were asked to rate eleven principal corporate functions in terms of their value contribution to the overall company. Sales received the highest aggregate score. Yet the surveys also showed that millions of dollars in potential revenue were being lost as a result of critical human performance issues surrounding sales. (The performance issues included a lack of motivation and selling skills stuck in mediocrity.)

However, sales managers—and, more important, the sales organizations they are trying to motivate—place a desire for training near the top of their wish lists. As part of the research for this book, we talked to senior managers and executives at leading companies in many sectors. Many of them mentioned the significance of understanding customers and aligning one's business operations around that understanding.

One top sales manager said the basis of his approach is to "understand what others want." Another noted the importance of "strong face time with the customer" and "translating our objectives into something that meets the customer's needs." A third told us his biggest frustration is "not being able to spend enough time with the customer." A fourth mentioned that one of the main reasons his company sometimes loses new hires to other companies within the first year is that, outside a five-week operations training process, there is no formal sales training or on-the-job support.

Another manager believed an effective way to inspire and develop a customer sales leader is to engender an ownership mentality, in which the salesperson comes to see the company as her own and sells it as though selling her own business. Yet without internal training, organization-wide support of sales or company alignment around customer needs, how can a customer sales leader act as an ambassador for the company?

Many company leaders have come to understand the importance of the sales function. In their decision to focus on the customer, they have decided to invest in the people responsible for direct customer interaction. They recognize that fostering customer development skills is invaluable; that, by training and developing salespeople and coupling that training with live practice and opportunity for failure, they can inch strategically closer to their customers; that training in customer business development—"sales" training—applies not just to those whose titles include the word "sales" but to all people in all functions.

Teach people their roles, train them and inform them about the customer, and there is no end to what they might accomplish; thrust them into an unfamiliar role, with no training, no warning and no knowledge, and they are more likely to freeze than to flourish.

Good Customer Relations

Industry giant Procter & Gamble is an example of a company that exhibits the readiness to change in response to shifting customer needs. Even today, with many of its products dominating market share, the company is examining entire business functions and activities within those functions to stay rigidly focused on customers' inclinations and desires.

Until recently, most of P&G's supply-chain improvements were internally focused and aimed at cutting costs. The increasing complexity of the marketplace has impelled the company to develop "sense-and-respond" methods, whose collective goal is to better understand customer wishes so that product response time can be nearly instant. P&G endures because it understands where its bread is buttered—at customer level.

One company we spoke with, a leader in the global food services industry, seeks to understand its customers' needs as intimately as possible and to fill those needs through a sales organization completely knowledgeable about its own offering. When asked to name the company's top three sales attributes, one regional vice president says: "One, a great understanding of our company. Two, a great understanding of the competition. Three, a great understanding of the customer. Championship salespeople know the customer's needs and marry those with our processes. They recognize the need to listen to the customer, think about how [the company's] offering meets its goals, and then connect the dots."

The manager gives an example: one attentive sales executive who, preparing for a call, reflected on what he knew about the customer, sized up the key points necessary to communicate, then reduced the sixty-page PowerPoint deck he had originally prepared to fifteen slides that directly addressed the customer's situation. The slide presentation hit the bullseye; the customer felt the sales executive knew its needs precisely and was won over.

We asked this manager to explain the selling process he encourages in his sales leaders. "Step one," he says, "is to know [our company's] business inside-out and how it fits into the customer's current situation. Step two is to listen—listen to learn what the needs are and how our products might fill them. Step three is to learn something new about the buyer every time you meet."

Another regional VP told this story: "Recently I went on a call with one of our representatives from headquarters. He proceeded to take out a seventy-two-page PowerPoint presentation. Forty pages were covered before one question was asked about the people being presented to." He believes the reason for this erroneous approach is a lack of practical training, which would enable sales leaders to interact effectively with customers, and a lack of theoretical training, which would teach them to emphasize topics the customer will be most interested in. Untrained salespeople can certainly be forgiven if they follow the instinct to push the company's agenda or if they think selling is about telling.

Jim Dickie, a partner at CSO Insights, a Boulder-based sales and marketing research firm, says real customer knowledge can be found not within piles of data but in the minds of those who know the customers best.[1] In other words, no amount of spreadsheets, analyses or flowcharts can take the place of one live conversation with a potential—or existing—customer.

Companies dedicated to training aspiring championship salespeople understand the difference between a high volume of customer calls and calls that are productive. When customer sales leaders make rapid-fire calls without obtaining knowledge about those customers, the result is stagnancy at best, regression at worst. The more unsuccessful calls a salesperson experiences, the more he or she may feel pressured to make an even greater number, imagining the odds will eventually turn in his or her favor. Championship selling relies not on odds, hit and miss, or trial and error. It relies instead on the powerful concept of knowing the customer.

So How Am I Doing?

With the need for training and developing salespeople goes the need for measurement and evaluation. Companies that invest in teaching people how to sell are also investing in measuring their performances. These organizations train their salespeople on the key characteristics driving customer retention. They evaluate how well the salespeople deliver against those characteristics. Most significant, they reject the transactional "call quota" mentality, in which salespeople are asked to meet a certain number of calls per day. Instead they look for call quality. Too often we have seen companies reward numbers of sales calls and pay no heed to the quality contained within those calls or the value they create.

---

[1] "Smarter Selling," *Sales & Marketing Management*, 2004.

In devoting resources to measuring business-building skill, these companies acknowledge three crucial interrelated facts. First, without being trained in understanding the customer, the salesperson, at a certain point, will falter. (What good are even the most effective tools if one doesn't know how to use them? The best hammer in the world is useless in the hands of an unskilled carpenter.) Second, given training, a salesperson can thrive only with support from the whole organization. Third, without criteria against which a salesperson can be measured and rewarded, the salesperson will not know how to improve.

Before an organization can respect and support its ambassadors on the customer front line, before it can make use of effective training and assessment, before senior leaders can connect effectively with the sales organization, it must be clear that those being placed on the front both want to be there and recognize where they are being positioned. In many companies, we observe unconstructive results driven by an antiquated model in which, seeking the best and the brightest, the company pursues and recruits top graduates without a particular role in mind, then slots them into sales—to their enduring dismay.

Companies might take a lesson from a leading global marketing services company in Canada that has built a successful sales culture in part by beginning all its recruiting efforts with two essential questions: first, "Do you understand this interview is for a sales position?" and second, "Is selling something you like and want to do as a career?" The efforts of this organization to integrate and support its sales organization are fittingly directed, willingly received and enthusiastically applied by budding championship salespeople happy and proud to be in their roles.

THE SALES TRANSFORMATION

In the past, salespeople were seen by the corporate world as transactionally minded. Today, they are being quickly made over into the mediums of greatest value to both customers and their own organizations. Those companies committed to riding, rather than resisting, the winds of corporate change are maximizing the talents of their aspiring championship salespeople to strengthen and expand customer links.

The old perception of sales was typified by Willy Loman, American theater's embodiment of failure and disappointment, or perhaps by the handful of distasteful characters in the film *Glengarry Glen Ross*, in which even the most redeeming salesmen are portrayed as desperate losers or compassionless cheats. Within the current stage of evolution, salespeople are movers and shakers who hold the most influential positions in business.

Companies at the forefront of business recognize and support those within the sales function with significant resources, formal training and constructive evaluation. Those organizations lagging behind need to adopt a fresh mindset, different processes and new disciplines whose collective goal is two-pronged: to make the organization-wide shift from a transactional to a championship perspective, and to empower those on the front to become champion salespeople. We are on the cusp of a new business revolution in which visionary companies will realize that success means docking the ship alongside the customer and having its emissaries disembark frequently to ask what that customer wants, needs and feels. Those companies who adjust the ship's course and empower their individual messengers will forge ahead, charting new waters, making new discoveries and establishing new partnerships. Those who maintain a traditional course will be left bobbing harmlessly on the wake.

CHAPTER 3

Changing the Focus

The only way to know how customers see your business is to look at it through their eyes.

—Daniel R. Scroggin

In recent years, companies have stripped functions, downsized operations and repurposed employees in numerous ways. The ultimate fault built into such acts is that they are essentially counterproductive—at best stopgaps, at worst inadvertent eddies in a continuing downward spiral. Winning with customers today means creating and communicating value through the skills and insights of those on the front line, who must be supported by all company functions.

Two steps are necessary to achieve this goal. The first is to adopt a truly customer-centric approach, pivoting the operation until it faces the customer head-on. The second is to weave the goal of business building throughout the enterprise; every function must become part of a chain that serves the goal of customer value.

THE CHAMPIONSHIP ORGANIZATION: BECOMING—AND STAYING—CUSTOMER-CENTRIC

Many organizations have achieved success through efficient manufacturing or judicious supply-chain management. Greater heights can be achieved through the transformation to championship alignment with customers.

The difference is this. Non-championship organizations, though often profitable and publicly well regarded, operate according to their stated goals and milestones. Every function is aligned accordingly, every initiative set in motion to pursue some item on the organizational checklist. A championship enterprise, by contrast, has made the collective decision to focus its operations outward based on the simple—but potent—principle of proactively aligning the company's offering to the customer's needs as closely as possible. We call this principle Strategic Customer Management (discussed in detail in Part Two). Strategic Customer Management contrasts directly with the transactional method of reactively trying to fit—or, often, force-fit—the organization's products or services into the customer's current situation.

Even successful companies that maintain a transactional approach can fulfill enormous potential by beginning to orient themselves outward. The way to win in the current marketplace is to step into the customer's shoes, and to demonstrate a keen

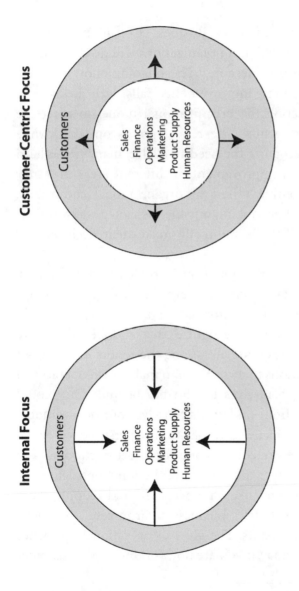

Internal Focus

Customers

Sales
Finance
Operations
Marketing
Product Supply
Human Resources

Customer-Centric Focus

Customers

Sales
Finance
Operations
Marketing
Product Supply
Human Resources

© Optimé International Inc.

Figure 3.1: Internal Focus vs. Customer-Centric Focus

awareness of both its specific requirements and how to fulfill them.

The aforementioned IBM Business Consulting Services study outlines key capabilities organizations will need to remain competitive in the next decade. [1] The ongoing effort to make incremental operations improvements falls well below the importance of altering the organizational model to meet the evolving customer agenda. The report points out that, while most companies recognize the need to evolve, many try so hard to drive incremental improvement in different areas that they succeed only in getting mired in organizational complexity. Instead, they should be looking outside their own walls to their customers—who, after all, indirectly make their decisions for them.

Understanding what is going on in the customer's head is, in fact, more important than it has ever been, since the average customer is fielding more information than at any point in the past. Companies that recognize this and become more customer-centric in response are seeing the results in improved top lines. Organizations that continue to make small operational improvements see themselves fall further behind. They could gain tremendously from nudging themselves out of traditional orientation and into a true customer-centric perspective.

This perspective stretches beyond the effort to cut costs. On the surface, it seems logical to improve the functions delivering operational excellence, like finance, IT and supply-chain management. But in today's business environment, this tactic often fails to deliver results. The glow of operational excellence has had its heyday; today, if you are not working on the customer

---

[1] *Consumer Products 2010: Executing to Lead in a World of Extremes,* IBM Institute for Business Value, IBM Business Consulting Services, 2004.

agenda, it matters little how well you streamline internal operations.

> When Bob, an account executive, is called upon to help launch his organization's initial "customer-focused team" for a very important customer—a leading mass merchant—he's both flattered and excited. It's a fantastic opportunity, and Bob is ready to deliver.
>
> Then Bob meets the customer's buyer, Ralph, who used to be a VP. "I hope you don't think for a minute you're going to bring any value here," says Ralph. "There isn't anything you can teach me about how to grow my business that I don't already know."
>
> Bob knows through the company grapevine that Ralph was demoted because of an indiscretion. He realizes Ralph is probably getting flak from all sides—he likely feels knocked down a peg and wants to take it out on someone. Bob knows customer-centricity includes devising specific strategies to strengthen individual customer relationships. He shifts gears.
>
> He asks Ralph to name the core deliverables he wants to meet in the next twelve months. Suspiciously, Ralph asks Bob what he is proposing. Bob says he will make a personal commitment to help exceed Ralph's goals, as a way to help Ralph regain status and respect.
>
> Ralph lists his core metrics, his top five priorities for the categories he manages, the specific deliverables he is responsible for and the percentage of those deliverables Bob's company typically contributes. Bob builds an extensive scorecard using point-of-sale data to show how each of his company's SKUs (stock keeping units) is performing week by week at each of

the customer's thousands of stores across the United States.

Bob and Ralph meet regularly. Using Bob's scorecard, they monitor product performance against specific goals in sales, retail distribution and promotional effectiveness. Bob points out where Ralph is underpurchasing or overpurchasing and helps him adjust inventory and allocation to strategically grow his category. Using the scorecard, they deduce that it would be more effective to promote the entire category rather than individual brands, and that they should do so immediately before Thanksgiving so that by the time people head out to do Christmas shopping, they'll have stocked up on the specific products in Ralph's category.

The strategy works—to an astounding degree. Ultimately, the scorecard Bob developed becomes a company benchmark. But he knows this isn't the most important win. What matters most is that, in demonstrating his specific commitment to Ralph's particular goals and by earning his trust at a fundamental level, Bob has cemented a vital customer relationship that will pay dividends for a long time to come.

The Power of Give and Take

While the instinct for individual survival and advancement may be biologically hardwired, the pursuit of mutual progress—the core concept underlying championship selling—speaks to an even more sophisticated human instinct: the value of reciprocity.

At our most basic level, we all subscribe to the belief that one good turn deserves another. Often, this championship thinking leads an organization—or even an entire country—to act in extraordinary ways.

In 1985, Robert B. Cialdini, author of *Influence: Science and Practice*, was intrigued to learn of a $5,000 donation made by the Ethiopian Red Cross to earthquake victims in Mexico. At the time, Ethiopia's circumstances were bleak—its economy in ruin, its food supply ravaged by years of drought and war, its inhabitants dying by the thousands from disease and starvation. Its plight was well known to the rest of the world. Even if Ethiopian Red Cross officials could scrape together $5,000, what could possibly motivate them to send it halfway across the world rather than put it to use within their own borders?

Cialdini learned of the simple reason behind the donation. In 1935, Mexico had sent aid to Ethiopia when it was invaded by Italy before the Second World War.

As Cialdini writes, "So informed, I remained awed, but I was no longer puzzled. The need to reciprocate had transcended great cultural differences, long distances, acute famine, many years, and immediate self-interest. Quite simply, a half-century later, against all countervailing forces, obligation triumphed."

Organizations caught in the transactional rut have spent so much time aiming at the bottom line they have forgotten how to drive the top line. By contrast, organizations dedicated to true improvement have shifted gears and awakened to the essential failure of seeking to generate revenue through cost-stripping and marketing swell. They recognize that the transformation to a championship culture begins and ends not with themselves but with their customers.

Today's winning companies make their value obvious to the customer rather than keeping it hidden within an intricate operational network the customer never sees. To transmit value on the front line, championship organizations build a robust, dynamic, cohesive support network for those who occupy it.

MOVING BEYOND PRODUCT-CENTRICITY

Stagnant or backward-sliding organizations in today's world find themselves unable to move forward, often because they remain in a state of product-centricity. Product-centricity refers to a relentless inward focus on a company's operations or products. A company that is focused inward cannot build usable knowledge about the customer.

Product-centric companies are constantly trying to improve their offering based on what they think their customers want. They develop no true customer focus and therefore no true sales culture. As a result, the sales organization is detached from the rest of the company, left to its own devices to try to secure the next contract or order. But the sales organization deals with customers daily. So the company ends up detached from the customer, just as the sales organization is detached from the company.

The danger of product-centric thinking was illuminated by a recent discussion we had with the general manager of a major player in the technology industry. The GM reflected upon why his company had missed the mark on a major launch initiative. A new product was brainstormed internally, refined with input from those throughout the top levels of the company and completed in time to go to market. At that point, the entire sales organization was brought in from across the country to convene before the marketing team, who presented the new product and then, wishing them luck, urged the salespeople to go sell it. The

GM said that assembling the sales organization proved to be of little value, since the marketing team, while explaining plenty about the product, explained little about how it aligned with the customer. The same value could have been achieved by e-mailing the information. The general manager realized that, despite communicating reams of information internally, the company had created no external value.

We might contrast this situation with the recent product launch by an organization rooted in championship selling principles. Prior to officially bringing its new product to market, this company undertook a six-month pre-sell cycle: it collected input from its top customers about several key features and benefits of the product and overall category, then made several significant modifications to the product and to the way it was marketed. By launch date, the new product strongly reflected the needs and preferences of its potential customers and captured a significant chunk of the market within weeks.

In our supposed forward-moving age of technology-driven sales, it is easy for corporations to overlook the fact that successful selling depends only secondarily on the thing being sold. Paramount to the success of selling is the degree to which the salesperson can identify, articulate and meet the customer's agenda. Let's say I'm trying to impress my date. I press my suit, rinse with mouthwash, get a manicure, buy an arrangement of daffodils and compliment her ensemble the moment she opens the door. All this will do me little good if I don't know about her severe daffodil allergy.

Put another way, if a company continues to ask itself how to satisfy its own goals—and not the goals of its customer—the best it can hope for is a serendipitous match between its offering and the customer's objectives. Failing such good fortune, the company's salespeople haven't a leg to stand on.

In a product-centric culture, the sales function is seen as an unsophisticated extension of the company rather than a key part of it. Those in finance, mzarketing, IT and other departments feel they are cogs in a wheel, and that salespeople are passive recipients of the great work the company does—that the simple role of the salespeople is to take the results of this internal effort to the customer. This fundamentally flawed perception hinders the success of the entire organization, because the entire organization should be working as a collective to address the customer's needs.

Leveraging the Entire Team

Product-centricity inadvertently encourages all those outside the sales function to become armchair salespeople; employees believe they're out there on the playing field interacting directly with customers. Within such a structure, of course, only the salespeople are out on the field; everyone else is relegated to the sidelines.

To win with today's customer, companies must bring the entire organizational team onto the field in a strategic configuration— that is, make the sales function the most respected, not the least respected, function of the company. Companies need to integrate all divisions—finance, IT, marketing, logistics, operations—with sales on the company's outward-facing perimeter, where the customer lives. It is here and only here that companies today can succeed. No matter how superior a company's product or service, no matter how many research and development dollars have been invested, no matter how expertly coordinated the marketing materials or branding effort, optimal success cannot be achieved without making the customer first priority, and to make the customer first priority, the sales mindset must be embraced by the entire organization.

Championship companies have figured out that breakthrough business success is achieved when the sales organization is supported both in theory and in practice. The customer-centric view presupposes the company will use its best resources, across all functions, to help customers meet their goals and overcome their obstacles. The championship organization, aligned fully around customer needs, by definition supports its sales function at every turn—everyone, from the veteran CEO to the junior business analyst, upholding the creation of customer value as the prime imperative.

Today's boards of directors, keeping an increasingly close eye on the corporations they oversee, frequently express this imperative as a question: *How are you creating value with the customer?* The answer to this question cannot be, "By cutting five hundred salaries." The customer does not see inside the operation. Nor is the answer, "By improving operational efficiency." The customer's main concern is not how fast a company makes widgets but how well those widgets meet its particular needs. Nor is cooking the books an appropriate solution, since organizational performance is driven not by fabricating revenue but by exceeding customer expectations. With debacles like Enron, WorldCom and Adelphia forcing boards to be accountable for the numbers they release to the public, companies must shift their attention to the real reason they are in business: to produce value.

By maintaining a customer-centric organizational structure and mental approach, the championship company answers the question: "By learning the customers' goals and tailoring our offering as closely as possible." The mindset driving this answer positions such companies well ahead of their product-centric counterparts, which, buried in their internally driven assumptions and analyses, continue to ponder their disappearing market share without ever turning an eye outward.

In championship organizations, boards devote an appropriate level of attention to customer management issues—since, in any championship environment, customer-centricity is an attitude shared by all those involved in the company's activities.

Current research into the activities of boards shows that such diligence is lacking in many of today's companies, despite the fact that a good number of them pay prominent lip service to the importance of the customer, even integrating this notion into their slogans or mission statements. A recent study looked at seventy Fortune 500 organizations and found that only twenty-one had a "customer advisory board"—a group of senior executives from current or prospective customers enlisted to provide direct, ongoing dialogue transcending the static information of market research.[2] The study says such boards are a "practical, available and dynamic way for companies to stay in touch with their most important asset."

Most boards that ignore customers lack representation from the people who interact with customers: sales leaders. Another study examined the compositions and priorities of a cross-section of organizations and reported that, in a third of the companies, the sales function had no representation on the board whatsoever.[3]

---

[2] Ross, J.A. (1997) "Marketing Research: Why Not a Customer Advisory Board?" *Harvard Business Review,* 75 (1), p. 12.
[3] Robertson, S. "Across-the-Board Consumer Focus Is the Way Ahead," *Marketing,* November 19, 1998.

The cost of transactional selling, over time, is significantly greater than the cost of championship selling. Transactional approaches are short-term efforts to get the deal and run. A transformational championship approach requires thought, work and patience. The proverbial acorn that produces a mighty oak tree finds its corporate parallel in the championship selling organization, which develops and nurtures a customer-centric approach, thus planting deep, strong roots with customers that eventually become trees constantly branching outward.

Table 3.1: Transactional versus Championship Selling

Transactional Selling	Championship Selling
Product-centric	Customer-centric
Efficiency	Effectiveness
Narrow offering	Evolving offering
Static	Divergent
Supply labor	Supply talent
Few points of differentiation	Multiple points of differentiation
Bought Business (not sustainable; unprofitable over time)	*Earned Business (sustainable; more profitable over time)*

The work involved in creating a true sales culture and becoming customer-centric top to bottom, end to end, may seem overwhelming. The sales function has been pushed so far toward the borders, many of us can hardly imagine what it would look like at the center of an organization. We are used to salespeople looking in from the outside; it's hard to come up with a reason they should look from the inside out.

Companies on the vanguard embrace the logic that the sales function belongs at the core of business today. Sales represents the direct contact with customers, the way water coming out the end of a hose, and not the concealed network of pipes feeding it, nourishes a lawn. Transactional selling perpetuates the myth that those who sell are aggressive opportunists whose only goal is to get customers to fill out an order. But championship selling espouses the idea that salespeople do not simply fulfill an empty task at the back end of the business process. Instead they carry out a role that requires exceptional skill and dedication—one in which they should take tremendous pride.

The IBM Business Consulting Services study noted earlier recommends several specific approaches critical to business building and customer development in the years ahead.[4] Two skills in particular encapsulate the complementary elements necessary for building sales champions: first, specifically adapting one's offerings with a strong focus on helping the customer achieve its business objectives; and second, aligning the sales and marketing teams—and, by implication, all other teams—as integrated units with corresponding incentives.

Once these two harmonizing elements are in place, an organization has taken its most critical steps toward implementing a championship culture. Most important, it has laid the groundwork for true sales champions to come forward and help scale new heights.

---

[4] *Consumer Products 2010: Executing to Lead in a World of Extremes*, IBM Institute for Business Value, IBM Business Consulting Services, 2004.

CREATING VALUE THROUGH SALES CHAMPIONS

Inarguably, selling used to be simpler. Goods and services were more clearly defined; protocol for calling on customers was understood by both buyer and seller; companies tended to sell one thing, or one group of things, without thinking much about branching in other directions. The term "vertical integration" would have left most door-to-door encyclopedia salesmen scratching their heads.

Today, the process is more complex. As borders continue to blur, as companies continue to consolidate, as competition continues to intensify and customers become more sophisticated, more informed and more insistent on their particular needs being met, the average selling environment involves greater sensitivity and expectation than ever before.

Yet the requirement demanded of great salespeople today is the one that has been sought the longest: a true customer-centric attitude reinforced by true customer-centric behavior, the ability to understand what the customer requires so that a properly tailored value proposition can be configured against it. When companies and salespeople exist in a true championship environment, they do not just talk about customer-centricity, they live it. The dynamic in such organizations is cyclical and self-sustaining: all parts of the company value the sales function and actively support the members of the sales organization, who develop business and feed customer information to the company. Supported by a customer-facing structure and buttressed by organization-wide alignment around the sales function, individual salespeople are able to draw on all available instincts and resources to provide customers with timely services, delivered appropriately, with little possibility of accidentally missing the mark.

Customers today are assailed with one-of-a-kind products, special offers, act-now deals and can't-miss opportunities. Add to that the endless variety of ways they can be ambushed—from never-ending junk-mail flyers to exasperating Internet pop-ups—and one quickly realizes that the days of knocking on doors and crossing one's fingers that the person on the other side will need an encyclopedia are a quaint, distant memory.

The new-world customer is a discerning creature whose attention is short and whose energies are divided in many ways. In a true customer-centric, sales-supportive culture, the salesperson is not a loosely attached appendage, but instead an orchestrater of resources who consistently delivers products, services and solutions that meet or exceed the customer's needs.

Stoking the Fire

When an organization refashions itself into one that is truly customer-centric and sales-supportive, it complements the natural competitive fire of its salespeople by arming them with real value. Passion effects little change if it is not balanced by substance; the same can be said for value if it is not carried forth by someone genuinely driven to deliver it. The combination of the two, in a customer's eyes, can be thrilling.

Recently we collaborated with experiential training experts exper!ence it inc. to develop a new learning and development process called the Sales Championship, a competition in which real members of a company's sales team are thrust into live, realistic customer situations. Over the course of a full day, salespeople experience the challenges, nuances and complexities equivalent to working in a market for three years. With continuous personal and statistical feedback, coupled with the goal of producing the best results and earning the title of Sales Champion, these sales executives come to learn what they have to do to sell effectively and to recognize how their real behaviors influence their relationships with customers.

The inborn competitive streak of those who participate in the Sales Championship is evident. We are continually fascinated at how quickly participants snap into pitching mode and how impressive they are at it. Our training approach also reveals the distinct difference between champion sellers and those whose companies have given their salespeople only transactional tools. The former, confident in their organization's support and sales-positive culture, begin immediately to ask questions about the customer's situation and what they might do to improve it; the latter slip instantly into pitching mindset, barely getting out a question about the customer's circumstances before telling the customer about their product.

Over the course of the Sales Championship experience, those rooted in transactional approaches learn slowly to change their approach. At the beginning of the day, they don't understand the difference between people who want to buy yet do not want to be sold to. By the end of the day, they have hit upon the correct formula: the approach must be customer-based, not transaction-based.

Salespeople are, by nature, competitive; they embrace the adventure of the Sales Championship, the immediate feedback and even the potential rejection intrinsic to the selling experience. Like the earliest explorers, they are energized rather than intimidated by the unknown beyond the horizon, by the uncharted territory represented by unfamiliar people, places and things. In a championship culture, companies maximize this natural instinct by supporting and encouraging it from within, and their salespeople, in turn, run with it.

Supported organization-wide and furnished with comprehensive customer-facing intelligence, these individuals conduct their visits and presentations confident that they are rising beyond simple transactional goals. Their knowledge of the customer is thorough and specific. Their offering is aligned directly with the customer's specific situation and represents true value. The salespeople are enthusiastic when they make their calls, for they can make a tangible, lasting difference for the customer and the customer's business.

The critical, visionary premise guiding all championship selling—that the salesperson's goal moves beyond the simple completion of a transaction—matches the emerging importance of the sales function. Top salespeople are no longer those who can sell anything to any customer; they are those who can best understand and fulfill a customer's specific requirements.

It is the responsibility of companies and those who lead them to create conditions in which true sales champions may surface. Asking championship-inclined salespeople to succeed within organizations that remain transactionally structured is akin to asking a teacher to educate a class of students without a lesson plan.

Winning companies today understand that sales is a core competency and have become mentally aligned to it. Their salespeople are supported by an organizational structure that lends itself to deep customer insight and tightly aligned solutions.

We recently encountered an individual who liked his customers very much and was sincerely interested in helping them improve their businesses. However, he felt he was spending far too much time and energy trying to rally support within his organization to help meet his goals. His customer relationships were often intense or heated, and this was fine, since they almost always ended up in mutual agreement about what was best for both sides. But this salesperson was growing weary of the internal battles during which the organization did not move toward a customer-facing stance. He was exasperated by the inflexibility of his company.

This is just one example of championship-minded individuals who struggle against a company structure that does not support their objectives because of ingrained product-centricity. By removing the barriers to championship selling, far-seeing companies are opening new doors for their salespeople. And their salespeople, feeling informed, included and supported, are marching eagerly through.

CHAPTER 4

Building the Structure

*Quality begins on the inside ... and then works its way
out.*

—Bob Moawad

On the surface, championship organizations look no different
from other companies. They have finance and IT departments,
marketers and accountants, computers and flip charts, naturally
adept performers and people who try to squeeze as much
potential out of themselves as the company structure will allow.
However, the difference in composition and effectiveness between
traditional and championship structures is vast. And the results
each kind of company produces also differ greatly.

In general, traditional organizational structures act like
poorly conceived extraterrestrial missions. Extensive work is
done to plan the spacecraft's launch, maximize its efficiency

and perfect the crew's instruments. But once the craft lands on a distant planet, its captains send a group of minions out to meet the foreign creatures without telling the minions how to communicate, whom to approach or what to talk about. Or the emissaries are furnished with polished messages about the history and accomplishments of their own race without knowing whether their cosmic neighbors will understand the language.

Championship sales organizations, like their counterparts, also plan the mission well in advance—but they ensure its success by studying the foreign destination, analyzing its atmospheric conditions, researching its terrain, decoding its language (through processes we will discuss in later chapters), operating on the assumption that the foreigners are friendly rather than hostile and, most important, involving the entire crew in the attempt to establish effective lines of communication. Championship organizations generate valuable exchanges between sales organization and customer until the two communicate like old friends who finish each other's sentences.

THE TRADITIONAL ORGANIZATIONAL STRUCTURE

The structures of traditional organizations possess a built-in flaw that often prevents them from meeting—much less exceeding— customer expectations. Though all functions in such a structure contribute in some way to developing the value proposition the company ultimately brings to the customer, only one function, sales, is directly linked to that customer.

Championship sales organizations focus on customer-centricity. This focus is reflected in their top-to-bottom effort toward maximum connectivity. In large companies with extensive resources, each organizational function might be matched to a corresponding function at the customer's company. A supplier's vice president of operations or logistics would be connected directly with the customer's vice president of operations or logistics.

Deploying individuals function-for-function is not always a realistic goal. Yet the objective of optimal connectivity on an aggregate level is still upheld in any championship organization, no matter its size. This objective is sometimes achieved with broader strokes: related functions, such as logistics and finance, share customer knowledge and leverage it against the construction of a tightly aligned value proposition.

Championship organizations derive most of their customer knowledge from direct customer interaction at various levels—including the very top. In a championship culture, senior leaders know first-hand who their top customers are and what those customers are trying to accomplish. The leaders possess this knowledge because they initiate regular interactions with leaders at customer organizations. They know they play a fundamental role in customer business development; they also recognize that they, and everyone else in the organization, are integral contributors to the overall selling process.

The connectivity-based structure is straightforward in theory, though sometimes a challenge in application. Once the structure is implemented, its value is clear. The difference between a traditional and a championship sales structure is the difference between a group of randomly scattered Lego blocks and two neat rows of the same blocks ready to be snapped together.

The aggregate connectivity of a championship sales culture fosters two goals critical to successful customer relationships:

When the seeds of growth are planted at various levels in a customer organization, results occur at multiple levels, too.

Figure 4.1: Multilevel Connectivity

increased functional efficiency and enhanced creation of value. Let's discuss each.

Functional Efficiency

Traditional organizational structures are set up to deliver products in a transactional way; decisions and products flow directly downward through the organization until they land on the desks of people in the sales organization, who are told to go sell to the customer. In championship structures, the organizations' leaders examine what value can be created out of the relationship between, say, their operations and logistics functions and those same functions within the customer organization. (For the many companies still structured transactionally in today's environment, a shift to functional matching confers tremendous upside.)

Undertaking the shift toward a championship structure is beneficial, but a question still looms. What happens when a newly structured championship company calls on a large enterprise still structured in a traditional way? To let loose the full power of championship selling with a customer not yet on the same page, the selling organization must initiate connectivity as powerfully as possible by communicating to the customer that it wants to learn about that customer's needs from the most relevant sources, and that it is committed to delivering solutions that get to the core of the customer's deepest cross-functional issues.

Again, the concept is simple in theory. But it requires a potentially complex shift in mentality. A championship company may match its functional leaders with their counterparts at the customer, or it may adopt a broad-strokes approach. Either way, the results will be evident.

The point is not whether two Finance leaders—one from the supplier and one from the customer—meet. The question is whether the mindset of functional connectivity exists at all levels of the organization so there are lines of unity and enhanced efficiencies in the overall seller-customer relationship.

In many cases, the attempt at direct functional connectivity will pose some thorny challenges. For example, issues of compatibility may arise between the technological tools of supplier and customer. Who better to resolve such issues than the IT managers of the two organizations? This is only one example of the ways a functionally aligned structure enables both seller and customer to move in lock-step from point A to point B, and so on.

When it positions only its sales organization alongside the customer, a transactional structure acts like a single nail trying to hold up a heavy frame. The championship selling approach aligns multiple functions within the organization with related functions at the customer and thus increases the number of touchpoints, creating high levels of interdependency and customer loyalty.

> *Janet, the sales executive for a Fortune 500 company, is assigned to a major retailer. When she joins the team, she learns that they usually talk to eight or ten people at the retailer. These are top decision makers or people who indirectly influence decisions regarding the retailer's brands and products.*
>
> *Janet thinks this is a fair number of contacts, until she learns that the customer employs nearly eight thousand people.*
>
> *She and her team make it their goal to penetrate just one percent of the overall customer enterprise. They will try to increase the number of touchpoints*

from eight to at least eighty. From senior leaders, Janet learns how this goal is accomplished: by initiating functional match-ups with the customer, thereby increasing overall alignment throughout all levels of both organizations.

Over time, the effort allows the team to penetrate logistics and finance and, as a result, better understand the way the customer measures its business. Functional matching also helps the sales team develop a connection with the customer's IT group. Now the team can ensure that ordering, inventory and distribution run as efficiently as possible. The team next engages with HR and is able to uncover deficiencies and add value around succession planning and formalization of processes.

Janet knows she has learned a lesson that will make a difference to her entire career. The benefit the team has derived from solidifying multiple touchpoints is tremendous. They and the customer have become like interlaced hands.

It takes considerable time and energy to increase functional efficiencies between a championship organization and the customer's organization. A senior sales leader might question whether this investment is worth it in the grand scheme.

In today's business climate, with companies expanding their operations and changing their structures constantly, every type of sales organization must find ways to configure itself more strategically against the customer, and the most effective way to do this is through a versatile, multifaceted relationship carried out at various levels.

In Janet's case, multiple points of connection with the customer organization proved a major boon to the supplier.

When the customer needed to launch a joint initiative between logistics and IT to modify their shipping method—a shift that and involved millions of dollars—they assigned the task to Janet's company because it already knew all the players involved. Janet's competitors would have required months of preparation to execute the launch. Janet's company—having made the initial relationship investment—was able to dive right in.

Top executives at companies of all sizes and compositions would benefit from spending time in other areas of their businesses, not unlike a medical school intern doing rotations in the various disciplines to better understand the overall field. The typical senior executive can begin to build a championship toolbox by working directly with the sales team for a few days— or a week, or a month. Some senior executives may already do this with the function they came from—usually finance or marketing.

The Creation of Customer Value

In striving to land more and bigger accounts, increase profits and accelerate closes, transactional companies routinely forget an important fact: customers seek not just products that provide temporary solutions, not just answers to fleeting questions, not just plugs for momentary holes, but permanent value. A sales organization able to transmit true value through a well-considered solution validates nearly any investment by a customer. The moment that organization is seen as being focused on the quick fix or big score, its reputation takes an irretrievable turn.

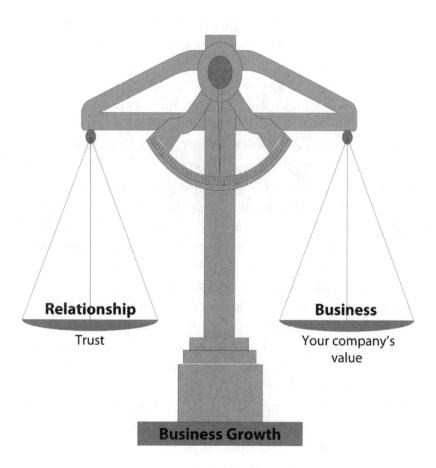

Figure 4.2: Relationship vs. Business Value

At some point in the customer relationship, if not at the very outset, companies mired in transactional thinking inadvertently convey their unbending focus on the sale. But a championship structure creates multiple pipelines between buyer and seller and thus enables the delivery of true value based on a broad understanding of the customer's internal workings and external goals. A transactional organization furnishes its salespeople with little knowledge, sends them into the fire and learns little from their narrow experiences with the customer. A championship structure, on the other hand, engenders conversations as deep as transactional conversations are shallow. A championship structure probes different parts of the customer's collective brain so it can understand the customer—the financial measurements the customer uses to peruse its marketing plan, the software platform, the distribution schedule, what new products it has in the hopper and what current products are leading the charge.

This accumulated knowledge allows a championship organization to provide solutions a transactional organization cannot. The transactional structure peers at the customer from across the room; the championship structure sees the customer under a microscope. The championship organization is always poised and ready to seize the next opportunity. It has aligned itself to deliver specific solutions to the customer in a swift, efficient, direct way.

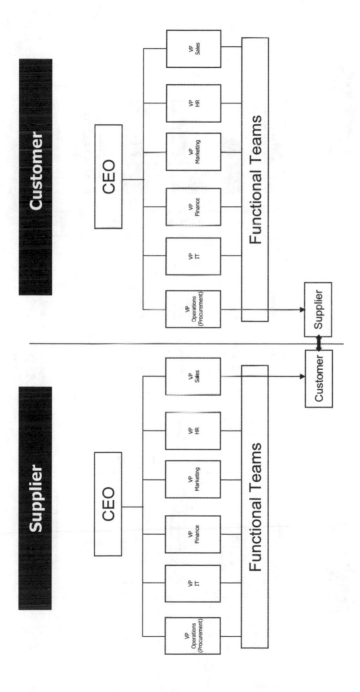

Figure 4.3: Traditional vs. Championship Structure

Championship Structure

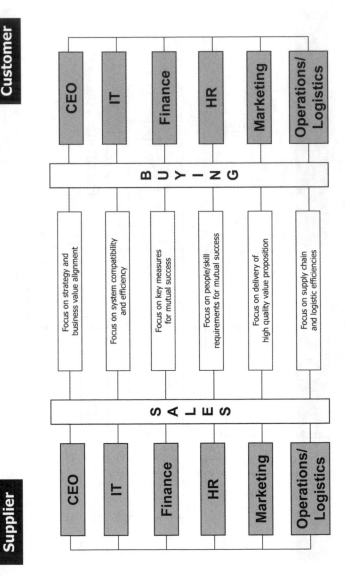

Figure 4.4: Championship Supplier — Customer Structure

CHAPTER 5

Unleashing the Power

You don't close a sale, you open a relationship.
                                    —Patricia Fripp

Selling's new frontier is being charted by those who have embraced its oldest principle: satisfying the customer first and last. Championship companies provide the groundwork for change by orienting themselves outward, creating a true sales culture within and creating the conditions for individual champions to stride forward and create customer value on the front line. These companies also achieve the proper balance between understanding the customer's strategies and adapting them to their own company strategies. Balance is important—companies that do everything the customer wants go out of business as quickly as companies that do nothing the customer wants.

The more complex the sales environment, the more powerful championship selling becomes. Companies that excel at championship selling seem to do so with the least effort. Like athletes trained so superbly that their performances seem natural, such organizations achieve the illusion of ease by spending so much time in their customers' shoes that those shoes come to feel as familiar as their own.

THE POWER OF CUSTOMER ORIENTATION

Companies that lead the way in the current environment— American Express, P&G, Wal-Mart, FedEx, Home Depot, IKEA—work painstakingly to give the customer a user-friendly experience. Such companies understand the harried lifestyle of today's average consumer. People are busier than ever, juggling more demands and responsibilities, trying to accomplish more in less time. As a result, the typical consumer values companies who can make the process of trade a little bit easier. This ease is valued more than product quality, more than low price, more than attractive design. Successful companies have acknowledged, in their structure, processes and goals, that the customer experience reigns supreme. As consumers, we don't passively acknowledge companies who smooth our buying experience; we get down on our hands and knees and thank them with devout loyalty. Ask yourself why you pay a little extra for the dry cleaner that provides padded hangers, or why you routinely drive a few blocks out of your way for sushi take-out from that restaurant that always includes a few extra pieces. Because, as a customer, your expectations are being exceeded, even if just a little.

Organizations that allow even small hiccups to hinder the buying process lose customers, and lose them fast. An organization that makes someone work a little too hard to find the product she is looking for, sells her something she can't easily assemble or dings her with a service fee the company assumed she wouldn't notice, will lose her to a competitor who can make the whole process a fraction less complicated. Put another way, the company has created a deficiency in services, at least in the customer's eyes—the only pair of eyes that matters.

The success of companies that have achieved championship cultures hinges on the ability to make people feel their needs are being met without undue effort. Many companies call this process "just-in-time" manufacturing. The term refers to a giant leap forward in productivity and efficiency, which ultimately translates into a hassle-free customer experience. This principle has been converted into dizzying success by Wal-Mart, a company whose value proposition is disarmingly simple: essential products at agreeable prices. How does Wal-Mart pull off its magic trick? The answer is no magic trick at all: they get to know their customers better than the customers know themselves. Or at least they come as close as possible.

Specifically, Wal-Mart has realized its extraordinary success by making available the specific items exhaustive research has told them customers need or want, rather than telling customers what they need. The company provides these items at comfortable prices and in a highly accessible manner, at the same time offsetting the innate transactional fear all buyers harbor—the fear of getting taken, of thinking they are purchasing what they need only to find out they have been duped by a slick marketing machine or a glib salesperson.

By placing customers' needs first, second and third—and investing up front to find out what those needs are—Wal-Mart feeds into the natural human inclination for buying and selling, allowing its customers to enjoy the process of exchange by stocking quality goods at low prices. It carries items useful to the majority of consumers. Walking through a Wal-Mart, customers never feel the company is guessing at their needs or trying to persuade them to buy something frivolous. Finally, Wal-Mart removes the sense of transactional bartering; the price is the same for everyone, giving all customers a sense of reassurance.

Wal-Mart takes care not just to meet customer needs but also to anticipate them. In September 2004, with Hurricane Frances barreling across the Caribbean and threatening a direct hit on Florida's Atlantic coast, Wal-Mart executives in Bentonville, Arkansas, wanted to fill their stores with products that would be in high demand should the storm descend. Following the principles espoused at every level of the Wal-Mart team, they strove to remove as much conjecture from the process as possible. They had examined buying patterns weeks earlier when Hurricane Charley had struck.

By using this method, the Wal-Mart team discovered that strawberry Pop-Tarts sold at a rate approximately seven times higher than normal and that the number-one pre-hurricane seller was—believe it or not—beer.

Such research is a drop in the bucket for Wal-Mart. Trillions of bytes' worth of shopper history are stored in its computer network, providing executives with information about customers' geographic proclivities for Snickers bars, lipsticks or jugs of antifreeze. The data are recorded item by item at the checkout aisle, then mapped and updated by store, state and region. Contained on Wal-Mart's mainframe database are 460 terabytes of data, about twice as much data as on the entire World Wide Web. This data, discussed at sales meetings every Saturday, are disseminated to Wal-Mart locations so all stores are on the ball and in step with customers. Wal-Mart also involves its selling partners in the experience, sharing information with suppliers via a private extranet called Retail Link. A company like Kraft, for example, can use Retail Link to inspect the movement of its inventory in various Wal-Mart stores.[1]

Wal-Mart uses its collected data to push for greater efficiency at all levels of its operation—from the front of the store, where products are stocked based on expected demand, to the back, where details about a manufacturer's punctuality are recorded for future use. And the company continues to raise its levels of success because it never stops trying to think like one of its own customers.

Championship customer-centricity takes numerous forms. It does not necessarily rely on data-driven insight into customers' most minute tendencies. Indeed, sometimes a championship organization is constructed around a single broad transformative principle that reflects a long-desired understanding of customers' needs.

Southwest Airlines became a remarkable success story, in an industry plagued by troubles, by delivering a value proposition that seems basic yet struck a powerful nerve with customers. Other airlines relentlessly bombarded customers with messages about safety, speed and efficiency. Southwest recognized that they were missing a crucial point: people wanted to have more fun when they traveled by air.

---

[1] Hays, C.L. "What Wal-Mart Knows about Customers' Habits," *The New York Times*, November 14, 2004.

The airline's overall disposition was represented in the smiles of booking agents, the jokes told by pilots and the pleasantness of flight attendants. The Southwest experience is highly affable, one customers look forward to repeating. When Southwest promised on-time departure, customers knew the company would live up to its promise; when it pledged that not a single piece of baggage would be lost, the pledge was upheld. Southwest's relationship with its customers is based on trust, sensitivity and, most important, understanding. Southwest's customers feel that the airline "gets" them, a feeling no company can put a price on.

The power of Southwest's customer-friendly model can be seen elsewhere. WestJet, a Canadian airline that just a few years ago was an unlikely upstart, has achieved outstanding results by replicating some of Southwest's example.

In the automobile industry, Lexus has accomplished a similar championship connection with higher-end customers by making them feel as if they are direct partners in the relentless pursuit of perfection. Lexus puts a championship face on the company. Our personal visits to Lexus dealerships reveal well-appointed showrooms boasting contemporary décor, waiting areas that include state-of-the-art televisions—even squeaky-clean repair areas. Lexus assures its customers championship service—for example, it provides loaner cars during repairs—as well as small extra touches, like a free car wash when those repairs are done.

On the surface, Wal-Mart, Southwest and Lexus may appear very different companies with highly disparate goals. At the core, however, the success of these organizations comes down to the same principle: they show how much they understand, and care about, what their customers really need.

THE CHAMPIONSHIP EFFECT

The tremendous achievements of today's customer-centric organizations demonstrate the power of championship principles. Wal-Mart, Southwest Airlines and Lexus show that the championship approach moves people beyond the instinctive wariness involved in a transaction—where we are as concerned about getting swindled as we are about finding helpful products—and engenders mutual gratification. By showing customers that it understands their needs and is willing to take steps to meet them, any company can find itself bounding ahead. Companies stuck in a transactional, product-centric culture only continue to run in place.

Yuri is the vice president of operations for a leading North American insurance provider. He is extremely satisfied with his team's performance. According to a reliable, well-designed internal scorecard, the company's quality rating is more than ninety percent— certainly nothing to sneeze at.

But something doesn't make sense. Despite the scorecard, customer retention levels are dropping. Yuri has talked to some of the company's top customers, and a startling revelation has surfaced: according to the customers, the company is performing at a less-than-acceptable level of quality.

Margaret, a company leader, asks Yuri and his team, "You're scoring ninety percent plus according to whom?"

"According to us," replies the team. They explain the rigorous measures and strict criteria against which they perform day in and day out. Every member of the

team keeps these goals in mind from the beginning of every project to the end of it. Collectively, they hit the mark with regularity.

Then Margaret asks, "Did you consult any of your customers, to understand their criteria?"

Silence.

Ninety-percent-plus of irrelevant criteria equals nothing in the eyes of the customer, someone suggests.

The operations team begins customer discussions. The customers describe quality components, and the protocol surrounding them, which are not represented on the scorecard. As it turns out, the scorecard is little more than a generic template that is applied to every customer, with no customization. The team is beginning to see things from the customer's point of view.

They create a revised scorecard using the knowledge gleaned from customer discussions. The new scorecard measures factors important to the customer. The insurance company, which had been in danger of losing its biggest client, can put itself in position to deliver at a level of customization and specificity its customers have never seen. The active acquisition of knowledge about its customers' priorities has proved significant to the company, and the application of that knowledge has proved invaluable.

Champion Entrepreneurship

When Thomas Szaky dropped out of Princeton University to start an organic plant food business, his parents were less than enthusiastic. When they discovered the product he planned to market came from worm waste and that his main marketing innovation was to package it in recycled soda bottles, their hopes weren't buoyed.

But the twenty-three-year-old Canadian got the last laugh. His product, TerraCycle Plant Food, was picked up by Wal-Mart Canada and distributed to its stores throughout the country. The product was also selected for store distribution by Loblaws and Zellers as well as the U.S. chains Whole Foods, Shop Rite and Wegmans. Today, TerraCycle Inc. is projecting multi-million dollar annual sales.

How did Szaky do it? By focusing on gaps in customer needs rather than on his own business agenda. With an array of jurisdictions across Canada either looking into or already banning pesticide use for lawn care, the market was ripe for useful organic and environmentally friendly products. "Everyone was doing it in their kitchen, but no one was really doing it on a big scale," says Szaky. "I thought, maybe there's something here."

As a true championship salesperson, he also knew that having a good product was only part of the solution. He needed to get it distributed—but the retailers he called were lukewarm. "We made over 60 phones calls to Wal-Mart," says Szaky, "before finally being given the opportunity to make a one-minute elevator pitch on why they should carry the product."

The high-pressure pitch was successful. Szaky was invited to Bentonville to meet senior Wal-Mart executives. And the rest is history.

CHAMPIONSHIP RELATIONSHIPS

Delivering in a championship manner means developing a mutually rich relationship with customers and making a tangible, perceptible difference in their businesses (and, potentially, their lives).

At the level of the individual, championship selling does more than satisfy business needs. It leads to mutual trust and shared accomplishment, which in turn produce fruitful relationships in which the best interests of all concerned are met without manipulation or subterfuge coming into play. At its simplest level, a championship selling relationship still drives benefit for both parties.

Relationships based on transformational principles endure because championship selling focuses not on the salesperson but squarely on the customer. True sales champions are defined by the way customers describe their relationships—as based on shared communication and continuous improvement. Sales champions deliver the company's value proposition with integrated, coherent support. Together these forces combine to provide the right product or service, at the right time, for the right reason.

> *Julie Lange is the investment advisor who runs the Belleville branch of leading full-service financial provider ScotiaMcLeod. She calls herself unconventional, partly because she uses only two main tools for customer interaction: a blank pad of paper and a paper calendar. She can make financial spreadsheets, detailed income graphs and complicated flowcharts available if the customer wants them. "I know other people in the same business use more sophisticated*

tools," says Julie, "but I like to begin every customer interaction with a blank slate, and having the clean piece of paper helps me do it. It reminds me that I'm there to learn about what the customer needs. I start every conversation by asking what this person's unique situation is and how I can help."

Julie is an outstanding success and maintains a loyal group of clients who look for excuses to recommend her because the same customer-oriented approach informs every aspect of her business practice.

She does the little things—says "please" and "thank you," shows up on time—and the bigger things as well—she will suggest that a customer go elsewhere, even to one of her direct competitors, if she doesn't feel she can meet the customer's needs. Like the most successful performers in any industry, Julie thrives by focusing on a simple but enduring principle: serving the customer's needs as closely and directly as possible.

Julie says she feels blessed to be able to deal with so many different people and learn so much from her customers. She also says she is the same person at work as at home, and the authenticity of the statement is easy to recognize. And she says that the transformational approach governs not only her business but also her life. She says it with passion and clarity.

Success, says Julie, comes from aspiring to be the kind of person who can say, after an interaction is completed, "I have truly helped the person I've just sold to." She makes sure her entire team treats the customer with as much consideration as she does. If Julie's assistant, Ellie, receives a call from a customer *who sounds not quite himself, she gently inquires if everything is all right. She may learn of anything from a sore throat to a death in the family. Ellie passes this information to Julie so Julie can be more empathetic.*

Julie understands that customers want to be understood and cared for. They want to participate in productive dialogues rather than one-way conversations. They want to feel listened to and heard, not tuned out. When Julie Lange is asked to name the key factor behind her success, she says, "Listening. My goal is simple: to find out what my customers need, to help them if I can and to do it in an open, trustworthy way. If you don't truly care about your customers, you aren't going to be successful."

TOWARD EXECUTION

Building sales champions—people who truly achieve transfor-mation with customers and within themselves—is straightforward but also challenging. It demands a shift in mentality that is, in theory, simple yet requires us to overcome our natural reluctance to embrace change. We have to apply processes and principles that are powerful but at first seem confusing. It requires us to focus on a clear, definable goal: customer needs. We must also align different people who have varying skills around that goal.

The psychological shift toward a championship approach may prove a major challenge, according to London School of Economics professor Tim Leunig, since the natural inward focus many companies adopt is symptomatic of a narrow perception of the value of buying and selling that has persisted over time. Though we may have an intuitive sense for the process of exchange, says Dr. Leunig, we often fail to recognize the power that lies within the process.

Dr. Leunig believes the championship transformation is necessary for modern business success. Some companies that execute this shift succeed in implementing transformational cultures, developing authentic sales champions and creating permanent value for their customers. Companies that have not undertaken the shift or have not recognized the need for change could still take the opportunity to pursue levels of success they may not know exist.

We have seen that the sales function is at the forefront of business in the twenty-first century. We know that recognizing this trend is key to corporate success. And we know an entrenched transformational sales culture can lead to true breakthrough performance. All this represents the why of championship selling.

Now, let us talk about how.

PART TWO

The Performance Pyramid

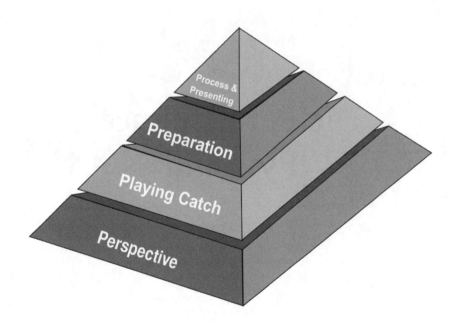

Performance Pyramid

CHAPTER 6

Perspective: Embedding Championship DNA

The greatest revolution of our generation is the discovery that human beings, by changing the inner attitudes of their minds, can change the outer aspects of their lives.

—William James

In our work we have tested the elements of sales training and development with tens of thousands of sales professionals in companies large and small, old and new, striding indomitably forward or fighting to gain traction. Throughout North America, our research has coalesced into a model of championship sales performance that converts the theoretical tenets of championship selling into practical methodology. This model aims to teach

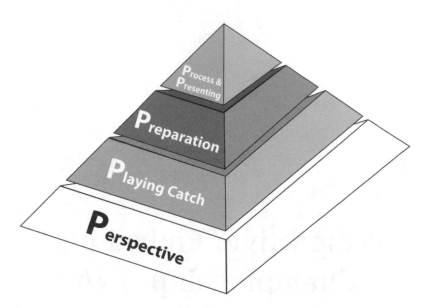

Figure 6.1: Performance Pyramid Featuring Perspective

sales professionals to win with customers in an effective and lasting way.

Our model, the Performance Pyramid, draws on three sources: decades of research into the factors most evident in predicting championship sales performance, our sales experience with leading global corporations and many years consulting to Fortune 500 companies on sales matters.

The Performance Pyramid, composed of four interdependent levels, has worked for companies that employ thousands of people and those that employ dozens. The framework is simple, though not simplistic. It represents the four vital areas that any championship salesperson or organization must master. Salespeople who focus on these four principles establish successful customer relationships that withstand the vagaries of business; salespeople who focus elsewhere often struggle to succeed. By understanding, embracing and practicing the four precepts of the Performance Pyramid, championship salespeople and their organizations ensure that their potential is fulfilled and that their ceiling will continuously rise.

In the top three levels of the Performance Pyramid we find detailed, concrete systems, processes, tools and approaches for interacting effectively with customers, evaluating their requirements and presenting specific plans to serve their needs. The foundation of the pyramid its most abstract level—is the most critical. At this level people confront their psychological framework and determine the changes they must make if they want to ascend subsequent levels. At the foundation, people face the daunting, exhilarating challenge of examining their own perspectives.

THE CHAMPIONSHIP MINDSET

What is perspective? Let's look at two salespeople, both confronting the same unfavorable situation: a customer who has said no. The first person is frustrated, distressed and resentful. His emotions incapacitate him. His confidence is shot, he falls into a rut and he can't find motivation anywhere.

The second person sees the rejection as an impetus. She chooses to analyze what went wrong. She channels her energy into preparing a better call the next time out and redoubles her efforts to understand the customer's goals.

In examining the characteristics shared by people who consistently succeed, we have found time and again that the most salient factor is how they view and respond to the things that happen around them—or to them. Championship performers maintain perspectives that breed success.

There are three prominent components of a championship perspective: attitude, emotional intelligence and belief systems.

Attitude

Attitudes are often described in dichotomous terms: people are optimists or pessimists, kind or mean, selfish or altruistic, utterly confident or totally lacking in self-esteem. Our attitudes are, of course, more complex than this, and most of us slide back and forth within the gray areas between extremes.

Champion salespeople place themselves at one end of the attitude continuum and work consistently to minimize backsliding. We can't overstate how the mental approach brought into an engagement can affect its outcome. Even if unconsciously, a negative attitude is always, on some level, projected by the salesperson and apparent to the customer.

What makes a championship attitude? The way we form ideas, approach situations and communicate messages is a complicated business. Is it enough to "focus on the positives"? Well, yes—and no.

A recent survey by research firm PLC showed that sixty percent of customers will buy a product or service after saying no five times. Yet forty-four percent of sellers give up after the first no, twenty-two percent after the second and fourteen percent after the third. Charging yourself with the goal of projecting a positive attitude certainly goes a long way toward championship performance. In the end, however, an optimistic stance results in superficial change. How does a constructive attitude feed a championship perspective? Why does a championship perspective have the effect of creating a fundamental and permanent shift?

Recent research by the Gallup organization into performers at Fortune 500 multinationals has shown that employees' attitudes can be slotted into one of three categories. Our experience with salespeople mirrors Gallup's findings. To appreciate the three classifications, one need only observe the behavior of participants at a typical sales conference or seminar. Two things are certain. All three categories will be represented. And only one contains sales champions.

The Jaded

There are invariably some participants at the sales conference who make a show—subtle or overt—of their disinterest. They are the people who find a seat close to the back of the room, remain resolutely unengaged throughout the conference, shuffle restlessly or check their BlackBerries. They make little effort to hide their lack of interest; they distract others with occasional murmured comments. They cross their arms and brace their chairs against the wall so they can lean back and let their feet dangle. Their expressions say, *I can't believe what a waste of time this is, I don't have time for this* and *How can that person presume to tell me how to become a better salesperson? I could write the book on sales.*

This group shares a classic glass-half-empty mentality characterized by a blend of cynicism, skepticism and general negativity. Those in the jaded group seem to focus on what is unsatisfactory in their lives. They are unable to express appreciation when things go well.

The Jobber

The second group conveys little feeling. They passively take in the environment as they arrive; they arrange their pads and pens, prop their briefcases against the legs of the table, settle into their chairs and prepare to listen, take notes, then go home. They might question the value of the event but will generally not voice their personal viewpoints except to echo the opinions of superiors or others with authority. Their nonverbal signals say, *This might be boring, but it's better than sitting at the office all day,* or *I wonder whether they brought in a good lunch.*

Such indifferent attitudes permeate other parts of their existence, as well. They get up and go to work for lack of a better alternative; they complete tasks without taking risks or rocking the boat; they go home at night, grab a bite to eat, watch the evening news, a sitcom, tuck the kids into bed, then do it all over again the next day. In general, jobbers see life as a necessity, not an opportunity.

Roughly half the individuals in a given group are jobbers. They're content just to put one foot in front of the other as long as they don't trip along the way. They do not feel they have much to learn or much room in which to grow. They are searching for meaning or resigned not to find any.

The Jazzed

The people in the third group enter a room energized, enthused and passionate about the opportunity before them. They're eager to learn, interact, share knowledge and develop new relationships. They sit forward on their chairs, alert, attentive, committed to taking their performance to higher levels.

This group is, of course, the one in which we find championship salespeople. The attitude they bring to a seminar, conference or training session is the same attitude they bring to every aspect of their careers. They are constantly seeking ways to expand their horizons and acquire new knowledge. They are never quite satisfied; they always want to nudge their personal ceiling a little higher. They want to make a difference to their customers. They're leaders who inspire the people around them to stretch with as much passion as they themselves do.

The desire to forge upward is an organic element of their constitution. The trait is called *performance drive*. The desire to be a champion comes from within. Champions are ruled by a competitive fire that tells them to play the game at the highest possible level. They are persistent in the face of adversity; they possess the instinct to push on when quitting would be the more comfortable alternative. People governed by performance drive are not necessarily the smartest or shrewdest individuals in a group. What they lack in innate ability they make up for in the desire to achieve.

Champions represent only about a third of people working in sales, but they're the primary architects of their companies' futures. The positive effect of these inspired salespeople on a company's success is significant. Companies have the opportunity to cultivate and develop these individuals, and to try to shift jobbers into the jazzed category.

Those in the jaded group pose a hazard: they pollute the attitudes of everyone around them, and thus lessen the effectiveness of the team. The jobbers warrant attention for at least two reasons. First, jobbers constitute a majority—there are twice as many of them. Second, the jobber *wants* to be excited by the job. Organizations that find ways to shift jobbers into the jazzed category will gain tremendous benefits.

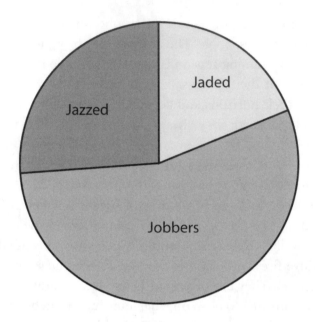

Figure 6.2: Salespersons' Attitudes

A championship attitude can be defined as unswerving focus on the potential for success combined with the willingness to create constructive solutions to problems. Such an attitude can transcend inherent ability and lead to continual improvement in the skills—both hard and soft—necessary for business success.

We talked to customers about what traits they value most. Asked to rank various characteristics in terms of the influence they would have over business decisions, customers of every type, in every situation, ascribed greater value to intangible traits than to technical skills. The implication is plain: while fundamental know-how and industry-specific knowledge are critical to sufficient sales performance, customers notice attitude.

Why do customers instinctively attribute such deep value to positive attitudes? One answer is that they recognize these attitudes are neither automatic nor universal. In fact, the ability to change behavior is among the most decisive tools for today's businesses, according to Dr. John Kotter, a Harvard Business School professor who has studied dozens of companies. Dr. Kotter suggests that the most vital levers for driving positive change often have less to do with strategy, structure, culture or systems and more to do with changing people's behavior.[1]

This imperative for change is equally significant whether at the individual level or in the context of an entire organization. When a salesperson adopts a championship attitude, positive change occurs; when that person's company does the same, change occurs at an even broader level. When both individual and organization adopt a successful attitude together, a critical piece of the championship perspective has fallen into place.

Building Positive Attitudes

The finding that customers value genuine, positive attitudes as much, or more, than they value the demonstration of concrete knowledge and skills has important implications for organizations seeking to inspire their salespeople toward greater levels of performance. Recent studies point to at least three ways in which companies can boost the attitudes of their salespeople.[2]

1. *Cater to the emotions as well as the mind.* Says Dr. Kotter, "Behavior change happens mostly by speaking to people's feelings. This is true even in organizations that are very

---

[1] Deutschman, A. (2005) "Change or Die," *Fast Company*, May 2005.

[2] Ibid.

focused on analysis and quantitative measurement, even among people who think of themselves as smart in an MBA sense. In highly successful change efforts, people find ways to help others see the problems or solutions in ways that influence emotions, not just thought."

2. *Celebrate quick wins.* It's important to identify and celebrate short-term victories or improvements for the vital emotional lifts they provide, asserts Dr. Kotter. Short-term wins, he says, "nourish faith in the change effort, emotionally reward the hard workers, keep the critics at bay, and build momentum."

3. *Challenge comfort zones while providing support.* Crossing the threshold into the twenty-first century, Xerox found its competitive edge slipping. The company conceived a new vision that required salespeople to change the way they had always worked. Their new mandate was to engage customers for the purpose of understanding the complexities of their needs or uncovering opportunities to provide them a broader range of products or services. At first, the effort proved unsuccessful—the company's salespeople felt ill at ease having to shake up their predictable routines. However, when Xerox increased its support for the new approach—for example, by providing better, earlier training and aligning its incentive system around the new model—its fortunes were reversed.

An often-prominent feature of constructive attitudes is the instinct to set distinct goals and diligently pursue them. A popular business tale holds that a group of researchers asked graduates from Harvard Business School whether they had created a long-term financial plan. Eighty-three percent had no plan beyond the immediate focus of getting a well-paying job. Fourteen percent had long-term financial goals in mind, even if they hadn't necessarily recorded these objectives on paper. The remaining three percent had written out a detailed financial plan with specific goals and timelines.

The researchers looked at the income status of the graduates twenty years later and found a startling result: the three percent who had in-depth financial plans were not just higher earners—they possessed greater wealth than the other ninety-seven percent combined.

Emotional Intelligence

In any occupation, hard skills, relevant knowledge and specific expertise are obvious prerequisites to success. Medical salespeople must understand human anatomy and the application of the devices they are selling. Mortgage specialists must have a strong grasp of personal finance and how their financial products work in conjunction with banking laws. Pharmaceutical reps must be aware of clinical studies and current FDA regulations.

Knowledge and expertise on their own, however, are often insufficient in the face of less tangible issues. We have all witnessed individuals whose laser-sharp intellect does not prevent them from struggling in a professional environment. What inhibits the potential of these individuals?

One answer lies in the concept of Emotional Intelligence, popularized by Dr. Daniel Goleman in the late 1990s. Dr. Goleman and his colleagues examined businesspeople in various contexts and found that the traditional measure of intelligence was not a reliable predictor of success. Goleman's research suggests that eighty-five percent of a person's success is attributable to her ability to manage her emotions. The ability or inability to produce results often has more to do with how we use our knowledge than with how much knowledge we have.

Consider the issue of weight loss. Many people have trouble shedding pounds and keeping those pounds off. On an intellectual level, most people easily understand the mechanism of weight loss. The equation is, in fact, frustratingly straightforward: we lose weight when we take in fewer calories than we burn. But most people who try to lose weight succumb regularly to their emotional desire to eat. They have the knowledge necessary for change but fail to apply it.

Championship salespeople apply emotional intelligence to themselves and to interactions with their customers. They recognize that different people have different dispositions, different motivations and different hot buttons. They try to adapt their styles to the styles of their customers.

Here are four behavioral types and the relational tactics emotionally intelligent championship salespeople use to maximize their interactions with each.

Table 6.1

Behavioral Type	Overall Traits	Key Strengths	Relational Tactic
Achiever	• Driven • Competitive • Fast-paced • Confident • Assertive	• Set high goals for themselves and those around them • Disposed to action • Constantly striving to improve	• Acknowledge and praise efforts and accomplishments • Make ready decisions • Maintain forward momentum
Communicator	• Extroverted • Sociable • Talkative • People- and relationship-oriented	• Forge relationships easily and work hard to maintain them • Work well in teams and groups • Adapt well to others	• Listen actively • Keep antennae up for salient information • Frequently play back main messages
Commander	• Controlling • Detail-oriented • Fact-based • Unemotional	• Highly organized and efficient • Willing (happy) to take charge • Rarely let emotions get in the way of sound decision making	• Bypass small talk to get to meat of conversation • Speak in terms of data and results • Be precise when using data and supporting material
Enabler	• Process-oriented • Analytical • Facilitation-minded • Risk-averse	• Nonthreatening • Even-keeled • Consistent • Personable	• Maintain composure • Demonstrate transparency • Consider all perspectives • Go slowly and steadily

Salespeople who want to develop their talents and the organizations nurturing this goal know that the ramifications of emotional intelligence reach beyond the context of individual interaction. A landmark longitudinal study conducted by Stanford University psychology researcher Michael Mischel beginning in the 1960s provides evidence that the ability to regulate emotions enhances the probability of success and is independent of intellectual prowess. In the study, four-year-olds were left alone to consider an interesting dilemma. A researcher would inform a child that he had to run a quick errand outside the room and that a single marshmallow would be left on the table at which the child was seated. The child was free to eat the marshmallow if he wished. However, when the researcher returned, if the marshmallow was still on the table, the child would be rewarded with a second to eat along with the first.

Some kids were observed doing everything possible to ignore the first marshmallow. They would sit on their hands, play games, run around in circles, stand in the corner—anything to get their minds off that marshmallow. Others popped the marshmallow into their mouths the instant the researcher had left the room.

Fourteen years after the original study, the same children were tested again. Remarkably, those who held out for the two marshmallows ended up significantly better adjusted, had stronger friendships and scored higher on academic tests. The children who had eaten the single marshmallow were more difficult to get along with, prone to getting into trouble and were, in general, less effective contributors to society.

The ability to understand and regulate our own emotions is a powerful skill. But for many people, emotions serve as obstacles to rational decision making—and thus to productive behaviors. William James, the father of modern psychology, said that when the mind and emotions are in conflict, emotions rule the day. Championship salespeople understand this propensity and work continuously to manage it. As a result, they constantly increase their level of emotional intelligence and conduct increasingly productive customer interactions.

Performers with championship-level emotional intelligence demonstrate four key characteristics that dispose them for success:

- *Self-awareness.* The cornerstone of emotional intelligence, self-awareness grounds champion sellers by providing a constant mirror into their behavior and its potential consequences. They recognize and understand their motivations and tendencies. Championship performers are aware of their hot buttons and the ways they interface with other people. Because they have an intimate appreciation of their strengths, weaknesses and opportunities, they are better able to adapt to predict how their behavior may affect other people.

- *Self-management.* Recognizing our own behavioral tendencies provides us with a baseline for emotional intelligence; the ability to regulate our behavior to achieve a goal dramatically increases our ability to perform at a higher level. Championship performers are able to regulate their feelings in the face of confrontation or disharmony. They are focused on maintaining productive relationships, creating mutually beneficial solutions and respecting others' opinions.

- *Social awareness.* Championship performers can empathize and appreciate viewpoints different from their own. They are conscious of how others might see things, so they can adapt their own strengths and talents for others. As well, they understand the underlying forces within their own organization and the customer's. Because they know how things get done and who does them, championship salespeople consider all factors before devising solutions.

• *Relationship management.* Champion performers can recognize and manage their emotions; they also pay attention to the forces that affect a customer's organization. They maintain effective, mutually productive relationships with people in both organizations to drive business forward. Champions create and maintain collaborative environments with their customers and place their own feelings and agendas aside to support positive change.

Organizations that seek to cultivate championship sales cultures must keep the implications of emotional intelligence prominent on their radar screens. Emotional intelligence can be taught, learned and increased. When a sales organization and the individuals within it clearly identify desired behaviors that yield desired results, then commit to developing and reinforcing those behaviors, customer-centric partnerships begin to form. And when individuals and organizations make emotionally astute choices that complement their functional skills, the biggest winners are their customers.

The Three Pillars of a Championship Perspective

Ray Lamont is one of the top life insurance salespeople in the world. When the top three percent of people in his field were invited to a roundtable dinner to honor outstanding performance, Ray was among the invitees. When a handful were asked to become members of the "Top of the Table"—the top half-percent of performers—Ray was one of them.

When Ray started selling for London Life in 1970, he wanted to know the rookie record for selling. His boss did not know, but he recognized Ray's drive and made up a figure—which Ray far surpassed. When we asked Ray the secret of his success, his reply revolved around perspective:

- "Understand the specifics of what the customer is looking for."

- "Listen to what the customer wants, needs and values most."

- "Show commitment to customers, and the rest will come."

During a call to a prospect who owned a pizza business, during his first year, Ray demonstrated such commitment in a way that proved unforgettable to the prospect. Ray introduced himself, and the prospect said a truck had just arrived and needed to be unloaded. Ray would have to come back another time. "That won't be necessary," answered Ray, and asked for a jacket. He proceeded to help unload the truck. When it was empty, the prospect told Ray to choose the type of insurance he thought best and prepare the papers.

Ray maintains the same positive, customer-centric perspective today. "I keep things pretty simple," he says. "Number one: I follow up on every lead. Number two: If I don't have the answer to a question, I'll say 'I'll get back to you' rather than make it up. Finally, I always remember that, in the end, it's about people interacting with people."

Belief Systems

There is no stronger influence on our behavior than what we believe—about ourselves and about the world. As we gather information and opinions from our experiences, we make decisions about who we are and what we can accomplish. We create a mental model for ourselves, informed by countless individual episodes and experiences.

Each experience is a small building block. The blocks are layered in a sometimes conscious, often unconscious fashion. Over the years, thousands of discrete moments—a teacher reprimanding us in elementary school, causing shame; a friend complimenting our haircut, making us feel glad; a colleague questioning our strategy, causing a threat; positive feedback from a superior, providing validation—form a complex and resilient structure we refer to as self-perception.

The internal structure we develop influences how we perceive and interpret the world around us. Over time, our self-perception resolves into a well-defined set of beliefs. We carry these beliefs around with us, and they affect virtually every decision we make. The more embedded our beliefs, the more information is required to budge them. If you are told time and again that you are absentminded, you may forever shy away from roles that require superior focus. If you have been traumatized by a dysfunctional relationship, you might seek a job that requires minimal personal interaction.

A belief system can form as a result of cumulative associations (someone who finishes in the black on three consecutive trips to Las Vegas may come to believe she is "good at gambling") or pivotal moments that shift a belief in a lasting way (a victim of abuse may decide that all people are untrustworthy). The evolution of our belief system plays a significant role in determining how much we think we can achieve. Left unchallenged, our beliefs can keep us from moving beyond certain levels of personal progress or professional success. They can paralyze our abilities and confine our thinking. We might stay bound to a certain level of performance or achievement because of a set of beliefs that convince us we belong there.

To change our belief system, we must see ourselves as dynamic, changeable beings rather than creatures whose traits, behaviors and abilities are unchangeable. The salesperson who believes she "doesn't do numbers well" must shake up her belief system by learning them. Someone who is habitually late for meetings need not remain "that person who's always late." He can adopt time-management techniques that change his behavior and his *belief* about his behavior.

History shows us how difficult it can be to force a shift in belief systems, especially those that have been long ingrained or are upheld by great numbers of people. For centuries, the most powerful and respected individuals in the world held fast to the idea that the earth was flat and that the sun and other planets revolved around it. This belief was so entrenched, and believed to be so unchallengeable, that anyone who presumed to contradict it … well, you know what happened to them. Ultimately, however, because of the staunch conviction of a handful of individuals whose nature was to challenge accepted beliefs, the assumed truth was proven false.

Championship people in all walks of life question and challenge their own belief systems and the beliefs of others. They test the status quo and push themselves beyond perceived limits. They try new things, gauging results along the way so they can build new beliefs and new possibilities. They do not hold past beliefs as immutable; they do not let past beliefs determine future behaviors. The outcome is constant personal growth and ongoing professional evolution.

Consider the experience of learning to ride a bicycle. Before we learn to ride, the thought of staying balanced on a two-wheeler seems overwhelming. Through persistence (and lots of prodding from our parents), we are able finally to climb onto that bike, overcome our fears and go sailing down the street. In an instant, our world is transformed. We've suddenly gone from walking to zipping around the neighborhood at breathtaking speeds.

Perhaps your particular crescendo of achievement came in high school, when the rules of trigonometry suddenly made sense. Or when the acceptance letter arrived from the university you thought you had no chance of getting into. Such moments prove to us that we can accomplish things our previous belief system told us were unlikely or impossible.

As we live, we ascribe causes to our circumstances. Sometimes we attribute events in our lives—positive or negative—to forces outside ourselves. When we do this, we are, according to psychologists, submitting to an external "locus of control." People who operate within an external locus of control feel the world is acting upon them; they are passive recipients of outcomes determined by external forces. When a person with an external locus of control receives a speeding ticket, the cop was looking to meet a quota.

Championship salespeople have an internal locus of control. They see their achievements and failures as outcomes of their own actions. It's often hard to adopt this outlook. But an internal locus of control enables us to continually evolve and progress. It's true that some events clearly occur beyond the limits of our own control. But we alone have the ability to decide what such events mean to us. We can change our perceptions of events—and we can change how we behave in the future. The championship belief system says that getting a speeding ticket is the result of driving too fast. By driving more slowly, we can avoid the speeding ticket.

Those with a championship perspective question assumptions and consider new information objectively before adding to an existing belief block. They constantly challenge and explode their own belief systems as a way to increase their effectiveness. They seek to grow and develop. They choose not to lament what cannot be changed. They believe not only that they can accomplish great things today, but also that they can accomplish new things tomorrow.

A Little Belief Goes a Long Way

In 2004, an innovative sales development firm, The Sales Activator®, and Nightingale-Conant, the world's largest publisher in business and personal achievement audio tapes, collaborated on a study of over 2,500 sales organizations to determine the five most common issues preventing organizations from achieving continual sales growth. One of the five issues identified was self-limiting beliefs:

> *Whatever you believe you can do, you will; and whatever you believe you can't do, you won't. Like everyone, salespeople hold stubbornly to private beliefs about themselves, clients, market, competition, economy—beliefs that can have an enormous impact, either positive or negative, on their sales performance. If salespeople don't see themselves as providing value*

for their prospects and clients, they'll tend to approach customers in ways that appeal to reasons for buying other than the customer's genuine business need. This is what sometimes leads salespeople to act pushy (for example, pressing a customer to "act now" in order to get a low price) or to be too accommodating (appealing to a customer's interest in getting his or her way). It also can lead salespeople to unethical behaviors because they may try to sell a customer something that the customer might not need. If they don't take care of their clients' best interests, salespeople will fail to build long-term client relationships and lose customers.

Remember to train the mental muscle of your sales organization, as well as its hard skills. Self-limiting beliefs constrain performance, and poor performance limits sales results. Encourage aspiring championship salespeople to challenge their limiting beliefs. Implement specific measures to change their outlook. Build their self-worth. It matters as much as the nuts and bolts.

Organizations rooted in transactional thinking try to motivate their salespeople by setting double-digit top-line growth percentage goals. Senior leaders use scorecards and ranking systems to measure success.

Championship organizations, on the other hand, continuously spur the belief systems of their salespeople and challenge them to build their knowledge and expertise. They get the most out of these salespeople by motivating them to increase their skills—not their sales, but their skills. These organizations also provide training programs. They don't ask their salespeople to generate more business just so they can put more money in shareholders' pockets or satisfy the CEO's strategic plan. They encourage their salespeople to think as champions by demanding that they constantly enhance themselves and their abilities.

These organizations know that championship people—not championship packaging, championship products or championship technology—make the ultimate distinction in today's business world.

Effective belief systems ought not to be considered the exclusive domain of individuals. Championship organizations that adopt customer-centric sales cultures instill at every level of their operations and across all functions a positive, productive set of beliefs based on an internal locus of control. A company that suggests a positive, dynamic belief system to its customers will be more successful in establishing and maintaining mutually fruitful relationships over time. A company willing to change its beliefs based on new information and shifting circumstances can develop salespeople who are also willing to change. Such companies will have higher external sensitivity, more assured customers and relationships that only grow stronger over time.

Exercises for Developing a Championship Perspective

Developing a productive attitude, high emotional intelligence and effective personal belief systems requires great commitment and pays large dividends. Table 6.2 presents some tips to help you fix in place the three essential components of a championship perspective.

Table 6.2

Component	Ineffective	Effective	Tips/Exercises
Attitude	• Dwelling on issues • Thinking short-term • Reluctance to change	• Looking beyond issues toward solutions • Thinking long-term • Readiness to change and evolve • Personalizing the approach by asking, *What can I do differently today to make an impact?*	• Visualize success • Think about how to turn apparent obstacles or barriers into opportunities for growth or improvement • Envision the specific steps necessary to reach a certain goal • Ask for advice on how to solve the issue
Emotional Intelligence	• Disregard for influence of emotions over decisions • Impulsive response, in-the-moment behavior • Evaluating others' actions and behaviors in the context of one's personal values	• Awareness of one's mood and emotional state • Commitment to step back and consider before responding or acting • Evaluating others' actions and behaviors in the context of overall circumstances and external variables	• Discover your emotional hot buttons, inflexible paradigms or counterproductive tendencies and study techniques for managing them • Ask successful colleagues what techniques they use to monitor emotions, then apply these yourself • Before meeting a customer, think about potentially controversial or emotional issues that

			• might arise; decide how to deal with them calmly and effectively • When faced with a problem, seek a way, not *the* way, to solve it
Belief System	• External locus of control • Belief that ideas are fixed and unchanging • Permanent internalization of beliefs	• Internal locus of control • Belief that ideas are dynamic and evolving • Frequent questioning and challenging of beliefs	• Attempt to disprove a firmly held personal belief (to remind yourself of the false notion of absolute truths) • Say aloud, *If I continue to do what I have always done, I will continue to get the same results I always have.* Then ask yourself, *Am I happy with the results I'm getting?* • Think about specific beliefs you hold that act as impediments to achieving a specific goal; commit to changing the beliefs and the behaviors associated with them

It's a beautiful morning for a meeting with a major customer. Though nervous—this is the largest grocery chain on her roster—Margaret, an account executive, feels ready.

Every year the company's CEO makes a point of taking manufacturers through the store to assess how their products are faring. Represented among the current group is a mix of divisions, including laundry, food and household cleaning, and Margaret's division, health and beauty care and paper (including diapers). The account executives, unit managers and district managers from each division have come to deliver a positive report to the customer's CEO. Margaret is alone. Her unit manager and district manager, though not present, are fully aligned.

"Who's here from the laundry business?" booms the CEO as he strides in. The account executive, unit manager and district manager all raise their hands and proceed to the laundry section. "How does this area look?" the CEO demands.

"This section is excellent, Mr. CEO," squeaks the district manager. "It's serving the consumers very well. Business is good."

Margaret's stomach churns and her palms start to sweat. She reminds herself that she is confident, motivated, she knows her business and she is here to serve the customer's needs.

"Who is here from the food business?"

The account executive, unit manager and district manager from the food division raise their hands.

"How does this area look?"

"Well, sir," begins the district manager, "this is a great section. And thanks so much for your business."

Margaret is surprised by the district manager's comments; she can see opportunities for his company's products in this area. She continues to walk the store with the others.

"Who is here from diapers?"

Margaret, feeling a bit lonely and more than a bit vulnerable, raises her hand. The chanting in her head continues along with the churning in her stomach.

"How does this area look?"

"Well, Jim," she responds, to the surprise of her colleagues, "this area offers a huge opportunity for both of us to make more money. The wrong sizes of diapers are prominent and there are insufficient quantities of the critical sizes most in demand by time-starved mothers. You don't have the top-selling size available, and therefore you are encouraging one of your key shopper groups—moms—to look elsewhere."

The CEO does not look happy. Margaret knows she has just made a hard one-eighty from the optimistic, sugar-coated message of the district managers. She feels as though she is covered in sweat. The CEO leads her toward the front of the store.

"Stay here," the CEO tells her.

Margaret is queasy, thinking her straightforward approach, though it had felt instinctively right, may have crossed a line. The others continue to trek around the store while Margaret stands at the front like a delinquent student awaiting punishment.

When the walk-around has concluded, the CEO returns and says, "I want to talk to your boss about this issue immediately."

Unsure which is the issue the CEO refers to— herself or diapers—Margaret takes a deep breath, maintains her perspective and persuades herself to stay assertive. "I am the boss, Jim," she says, "and we both stand to increase profits substantially through some adjustments in this area."

The CEO stares at her for what seems like an eternity, then walks away, shouting, "Ken!"

A stock boy comes running. "This woman is going to explain some changes to be made in the diaper section. Make the same arrangements for all other stores in the region. I want this done by the end of the day."

The Five-Point Championship Perspective

We studied the behaviors of championship sales performers in a number of large corporations. Our research revealed five distinct perspective-related traits they share:

1. *Desire to help others succeed.* No champion salesperson exists who has a narrow or inward-facing definition of success. The highest-level performers consider an interaction successful only when there is reciprocal progress between themselves and their customers. It is the exception, not the rule, when championship success is achieved single-handedly.

2. *Ability to help shape others' thinking.* Many types of people can think strategically, communicate persuasively or devise creative solutions to business problems. Championship salespeople focus these abilities toward crafting a customer agenda that will lead to positive change and ongoing success.

3. *Willingness to take risks.* Championship salespeople want to be in the forefront of customer development—they want to go see customers, to leave the comfort and safety of the office, to venture forth into new and unfamiliar environments. They don't accept old paradigms; instead they strive to create new ones. They ask the tough questions to come up with innovative answers.

4. *Adaptability.* Championship salespeople win with customers by living and sharing a perspective of constant transformation. They adapt their style to the customer's; they do not force the customer to adapt to them. They address unexpected circumstances by adjusting while remaining focused on overall goals. When stuck at a plateau, they rouse themselves to new heights. Perhaps most important, new-world championship salespeople don't shrink in the face of complex customer environments or intense competition. Instead they remain adaptable through an outward-facing stance.

5. *Follow-through.* Throwing in the towel amid difficult circumstances is not part of the championship salesperson's vocabulary. Championship performers stay the course and inspire their customers to do the same. They maintain the staunch mentality required to produce when conditions are not necessarily favorable. They dig deep to find the passion and drive that keep them focused on key goals and milestones. Above all, they recognize that success is not a result of talent alone: it comes from talent combined with commitment.

Physical Fitness and the Championship Salesperson

The championship salesperson's mind is always honed to a fine edge when it comes to customer knowledge. She may spend days planning a one-hour meeting, bringing to bear all her intellectual horsepower and business acumen, pulling together resources throughout the organization, focusing intensely on top-line messages to be shared and information to be drawn out.

Championship selling, however, takes a lot of work, a lot of effort and, sometimes, extraordinary amounts of energy in the face of extreme pressure. To optimize their performance in these situations, true championship performers arrive as physically sharp as they are mentally.

Do not overestimate the selling power of a well-tuned mind; similarly, do not underestimate the potential effects of inner lethargy or discomfort on outer performance.

Follow the example of professional athletes when preparing for an important customer call. Drink water beforehand, not coffee; eat meals highlighted by proteins and nutrient-rich items rather than fast food or other junk high in fats and refined sugar; consume enough to fuel your engine but not so much that you get sluggish. A mind plodding slowly along trying to find its way through the nuances of a call will be obvious to a customer every time. But a properly nourished body will lead instead to higher energy, a positive aura, greater confidence and a finer ability to respond to the customer. The capacity to gather the correct knowledge and frame it appropriately for the customer is the key practical tool a championship

> salesperson possesses. But remember also that these practical techniques are more effectively carried out when the championship mind and body work together to form a faster, crisper, more flexible, more adaptable, better integrated machine for breakthrough performance.

CLIMBING THE PYRAMID

The tools and processes described in the upper three levels of the Performance Pyramid depend on having the proper perspective cemented in place at the foundation. Adopting constructive attitudes, managing our emotions and challenging our belief systems will create the solid groundwork from which we can begin to proceed up the pyramid. The second stage involves an activity familiar to many, though leveraged by few: playing catch.

10 QUESTIONS FOR REFLECTION: PERSPECTIVE

- Do I have a generally positive attitude about what I do? How do I demonstrate this?

- What is my level of Emotional Intelligence, and what might I do to enhance it?

- Is my belief system configured in such a way that I maintain resilience in the face of disappointment?

- Do I tend to consider new information objectively, or do I slot it immediately into one or another of my "belief files"?

- Do I have an internal or external locus of control?

- Do I welcome new challenges, experiences, opportunities and pursuits, or do I prefer just to go along as before?

- Do I spend more time on my sales "image" or on my ability to connect with the customer?

- Does my organization communicate a positive internal attitude? External attitude?

- Does my organization foster an atmosphere of Emotional Intelligence?

- Does my organization nurture a constructive set of beliefs about itself? About its employees?

CHAPTER 7

Playing Catch: The Heart of Championship Selling

*You can tell whether a man is clever by his answers.
You can tell whether a man is wise by his questions.*
—Naguib Mahfouz

To the casual fan it may seem a pitcher controls a baseball game. But people who possess an intimate knowledge of the sport know better. The catcher makes the critical decisions that guide the pitcher's behavior and the game's tempo; the catcher must be skilled at observing the big picture and the slight shifts in momentum; the catcher, more than anyone else, unobtrusively affects the game's moment-to-moment direction, and thus its outcome.

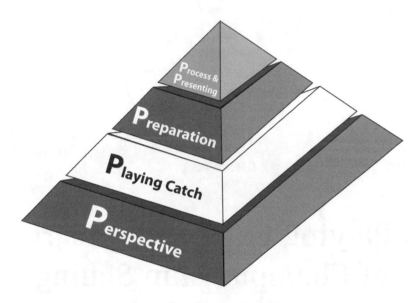

Figure 7.1: Performance Pyramid Featuring Playing Catch

So it is with championship selling. Several years ago, a client asked us what we thought selling was all about. Our answer represented a simple yet powerful concept called playing catch, and it continues to be our most resonant training concept and the principle that encompasses the second level of the Performance Pyramid. Let's break it down.

PITCHING

The traditional view of selling holds that great salespeople are experts at the "pitch"—they look great, talk fast and are naturally gifted at persuasion. Executives ask their sales teams if they have the pitch ready. Salespeople tell their colleagues they are preparing to go out and make a pitch for certain business. Managers prod their salespeople to become great closers.

When they are pitching, these salespeople are doing the same thing a baseball pitcher does: they serve up one offering after another, with few pauses in between, and they try to throw as accurately as possible.

And why shouldn't they? It is that figure on the mound, that thrower toeing the rubber, who is most easily recognized, most highly paid and most often lionized in baseball's annals. Most of the sport's fans can name, with little effort, pitchers who have thrown recent no-hitters or won the Cy Young Award. The pitcher is in the spotlight; the pitcher—literally—stands above everyone else on the field; the pitcher makes the first move and then waits for a reaction.

Relentless pitching, however, is a fundamentally unproductive way to move conversations forward or develop valuable customer insights. Champion sellers have learned an invaluable lesson that runs counter to the instinct to pitch: the more salespeople talk, the *less* they are in control of a conversation. And the less they are in control, the less they learn about and endear themselves to the customer.

Championship salespeople keep the urge to pitch at bay. They assume the role of the other half of the baseball battery: the catcher.

CATCHING

Of the many thousands of salespeople we train, the vast majority are startled by the realization that they spend the largest part of their time with customers pitching, not catching. When we reveal that catching—not pitching—is the essential principle in championship selling, they are taken aback, for it is in the salesperson's blood to pitch. Sometimes from a very young age, salespeople have been told they should go into sales when they grow up because they are good talkers. (*"Man, that little guy likes to talk. He should go into sales."*) They have been told they were born to sell because they have the "gift of the gab." We tell them they can become even better at selling by finding the "secret of silence."

You might pitch until you're blue in the face and never learn an iota about the needs of the person on the other side of the table. We see a compulsion to pitch in most salespeople. It's a result of their aversion to losing control. When they lack a pitch, they do not feel on top of the game. By delivering one pitch after another they feel they can prevent the customer from tuning out, packing up or shying away.

The problem is this: a pitcher, on the mound or in a boardroom, is focused only on what he is doing. To be successful, a salesperson must turn his attention outward.

Pitching Parodied

We don't have to look far to see the negative images of salespeople as desperate pitchers. In early 2005, the pop-culture institution *Saturday Night Live* reflected this perception in a skit: a handful of salespeople are shown in a training session practicing their delivery of a customer solution.

The first, a former military officer, marches to the front of the room and hollers "TYLENOL!" at the audience. The second, a woman terrified of public speaking, ekes out a string of unintelligible words before finally whispering, "Female protection." The third, a man afflicted with a rare condition that causes him to make inappropriate gestures, nervously delivers his pitch while unintentionally pointing to his groin or making punching motions. The fourth, the stereotypical slick sales executive, races breathlessly through a high energy, in-your-face, buy-our-product pitch that can scarcely be understood.

The *SNL* skit shows an intuitive sense for the value of catching. The fifth salesperson in the group—the only trainee to impress the rest of the class—is asked to demonstrate his pitch. He says, "Actually, it's more of a conversation." Bingo.

When we ask salespeople for their definition of a great customer call, some tell us it is a call in which they got the order by "nailing the pitch," "delivering all the key messages" or "hitting the ball out of the park." These salespeople are transactionally minded. In a meeting, they will pitch with barely a pause, tirelessly giving their spiels, keeping their antennae up for lulls so they can fill them, ensuring they talk through every slide in their PowerPoint presentations.

These salespeople learn little about their customers.

When we receive a response such as, "A call in which I came away with new knowledge about the customer's needs," we know we are talking to a champion seller. Such salespeople go into customer meetings looking to slip into a catching role as early as possible. They make it clear to the customer that their chief goal is not to pitch a product or service but to learn about that customer's objectives and to explore solutions together.

David House, a group president for American Express Worldwide, echoes this view. When asked to name the most critical skill a customer sales leader ought to have, David answers,

"Listening, asking questions and gathering information. In fact, on an initial call, I encourage my salespeople, if possible, just to listen."

The champion salesperson listens, processes, gains understanding and seeks insight. He is never waylaid by the need to wow the customer with state-of-the-art graphics or mountains of support documentation. By the end of the meeting, he may have said very little, but he has learned a boatload about the most important person there.

A catcher is focused not on himself but on everyone else. For this reason he absorbs more valuable information than any other player on the diamond. He is constantly receiving, observing and absorbing—all the while guiding the game. You may recall a scene in the classic baseball film *Bull Durham* in which cannon-armed pitcher Ebby Calvin "Nuke" LaLoosh, played by Tim Robbins, stubbornly throws fastball after fastball in an attempt to strike hitters out. His zeal and stubborn self-focus prevent him from acquiring new information or thinking strategically. He finds himself unable to move beyond his current level of performance.

Nuke's batterymate, Crash Davis (Kevin Costner), is a career minor-league catcher with deep wisdom about the game and its nuances. At one point, Crash jogs out to the mound and advises Nuke to make the next pitch a curveball. Nuke refuses, insisting he can blow a fastball by the hitter. Crash again suggests the curveball. No dice, says Nuke, the fastball is his bread and butter. Crash returns to his spot behind the plate—but not before telling the hitter a fastball is coming. Nuke deals the fastball, and the hitter, grinning, tattoos it, belting a home run deep into the stands. Crash visits the mound again, and Nuke says, "Man, it's like he knew that pitch was coming."

"He did," Crash replies—letting Nuke know who's really in control.

Juan is an experienced principal with a leading consulting firm. He is preparing to see the senior vice president of sales for a major potential account. Juan and Kathy, a consultant partner, recognize the enormous upside of winning this business, and they have prepared arduously to present their firm's capabilities.

Brimming with nervous energy and anxious to launch into their pitch, Juan and Kathy begin the meeting with pleasantries and casual dialogue to establish rapport. When the moment of truth arrives, Juan dives in, explaining how he and his team can significantly exceed the company's expectations for the coming period.

Less than a minute into Juan's introductory remarks, the SVP interjects. "Our company is a global industry leader. We deal with over 125 consulting agencies around the world. I'd like to know what makes you the best."

Juan is stopped in his tracks. His mouth goes dry. He stares at the SVP, hoping something profound will come out of his mouth. His mind races as he tries to think of a way to respond. He looks at his briefcase, where the carefully organized testimonials, trend data, videos and relevant examples of his firm's expertise lie awaiting just such a moment. The instinct to pull every piece of ammunition in his well-honed arsenal is coursing through Juan's veins.

His hand is inching closer to the briefcase. He stops himself and asks: "What criteria do you use to decide the best?"

The SVP, pleased to demonstrate his knowledge and authority, begins pitching. He explains the specific qualities his company is seeking from consultant partnerships and the particular objectives he wishes to achieve.

After more than half an hour of uninterrupted pitching, the SVP pauses, looks Juan in the eye, and says, "So—can you do this or not?"

Suddenly the elaborate presentation Juan and Kathy have planned is refined into two words. "Of course," Juan says.

"Excellent," responds the SVP. "When can you start?"

This story is true—one of our key clients was involved. In our training sessions, we like to tell the story to emphasize the concept of catching and the difficulty most people have resisting the urge to pitch.

There is a pattern we see repeatedly in our sessions. After two hours of talking about catching, sharing this story, watching the audience laugh and widen their eyes with recognition, we ask people to assume the role of Juan, the sales consultant sitting in with the SVP. Ninety-nine percent of the time, we see people revert to pitching.

Think of pitching as trying to communicate value based on current assumptions or old knowledge. Now think of catching as a vehicle for unearthing fresh insights and finding new points of alignment. When you pitch, you tell a customer what value your product or service can bring. When you catch, you interweave that product or service with the customer's goals or targets. More simply, pitching is telling; catching is learning.

Catching for Life

Whether you believe catching is a vital skill for business, try this on for size: those who practice catching live longer.

In a recent study[1] spanning two decades, nearly eight hundred men were assessed on their proclivity for "social dominance," characterized by behaviors such as the compulsion to control conversations or the inability to let others speak without interrupting, often for the purpose of selling oneself.

The study found that men who exhibited these traits were sixty percent more likely to die from heart disease or similar causes than those more inclined to let others talk. Says lead researcher Michael Babyak, "One of the striking features about these sorts of individuals is that they will perceive threats to their dominance in even the most neutral or benign settings, so that they will pounce on the chance to be in control even when it's not really called for."

So start listening. Not only will it allow you to interact more effectively with customers—you'll also be around longer to do it.

How Do I Know If I'm Catching?

It isn't always easy to determine whether you're catching effectively. You might leave a meeting thinking it went splendidly only to discover you've learned almost nothing about what the customer really needs—meaning you probably spent most of the time pitching. Sometimes you feel anxious because during

---

[1] Houston, B.K., Babyak, M.A., Chesney, M.A., Black, G. & Ragland, D.R. (1997) *Social Dominance and 22-Year All-Cause Mortality in Men*, Department of Psychology, University of Kansas, Lawrence, USA.

an entire meeting you did almost none of the talking. Then you realize you've left with a much deeper understanding of the customer's current goals and how to meet them—meaning you caught successfully.

Here are four tests for evaluating how well you catch:

1. If your catching instinct is well entrenched, you'll find yourself preparing questions for the customer in advance of a meeting or call. If you're having trouble resisting the pitch, you'll probably find yourself imagining the different questions the customer might ask you. During customer meetings, a chronic pitcher will constantly think, *What can I say that will make him want to close the deal?* The person inclined to catch will constantly wonder, *What can I ask to get him to talk even more about the company's needs?*

2. If you're effectively playing catch with your customer, you should be able to articulate, in the customer's language, its key strategies (including specific objectives for your individual contact), its goals and objectives for the upcoming year, its short- and long-term priorities, its overall value proposition and how your product or service helps the customer deliver all this.

3. Any time you ask questions or take a turn to pitch, it should be to add substance. Ask yourself how often, and for what purpose, you typically interrupt during meetings with customers. If the purpose of your interjection is to re-articulate the customer's priorities, confirm its agenda, explore its goals or explain how your value proposition ties in, you're probably catching well and choosing opportune moments to pitch. If you find yourself jumping in at

regular intervals regardless of what's being discussed or if you pounce on pauses because you're unsure who's supposed to go next, it's likely you need to practice more focused catching. Practice will put you at ease and develop your awareness for constructive turn taking.

4.   Think about how often customers say to you, "That's a good question," "I never thought of it that way" or "I never looked at it from that perspective." The more comments like this you hear, the better you're catching.

To demonstrate the power of catching, we conduct an experiment during workshops. Once we feel the audience members have begun to internalize the concept, we ask them to step out of the meeting room (yes, in the middle of the seminar) and call one of their customers with the goal of finding out something new. (The best time to start applying the concept of catching is always, "Right now.")

Often participants say, "I really don't feel prepared to do this." Some salespeople resist because they don't have time to prepare what they are going to say. They think, *How can I pick up the phone and do an impromptu pitch?* This reaction, of course, makes the point. The purpose of the contact is *not to pitch*, but to get customers talking about their needs, to gather new information, to gain even one tiny new nugget of insight—by catching.

Once when we issued this challenge, a self-assured seminar attendee, vice president of sales for his company, said he would demonstrate how to call a customer. He phoned the senior vice president of merchandising at one of his most important customers, a leading North American retailer. The SVP's assistant answered the call and advised that he was in a meeting.

Faced with such a standard rebuff, most people shut down. They offer conversation closers like, "Okay, can I leave him a message, or maybe you could have him call me?" The VP was up to the task. He told the assistant, "It's very important that I chat with him." The assistant said the SVP was, in fact, in a management committee meeting, but if it was truly important, she'd interrupt him. Yes, said the VP, it's truly important.

Soon the customer SVP got on the phone echoing the assistant's sentiment: "This had better be important."

The response of the sales leader who had initiated the call is a golden example of effective catching: "My team and I are in the middle of a meeting talking about your business and its importance to us, and we realize there are a lot of things we don't know. I was wondering if I could have your help and ask you a couple of questions so we can better understand your situation."

The customer's reaction? He told his management committee to take a short break.

After fifteen minutes explaining his company's key strategies for the coming year, the customer said it had been a valuable phone call, and that he could see why the VP interrupted him. He thanked him, in fact, for doing so. That year, the VP's company increased its business with the customer by twenty-five percent.

Catching to Stay on Course

Customer meetings are unpredictable, and you need skills to keep customers on track when they're threatening to derail. Catching helps you gather critical information about your customers' needs and objectives. It also allows you to gently edge them back on course.

Let's assume you're in the middle of explaining one of your products to a customer whose needs you feel match up well. The customer says she is having trouble seeing how your product will fit her particular requirements. Or, worse, she tells you bluntly that she has no space, the price of the product or service is too high or her budget is shut tighter than a Tupperware lid.

You have a choice: pitch or catch. Pitching would mean regurgitating what you've said, or saying the same thing a different way. If you're catching, however, you can understand what is preventing your customer from acknowledging the value your product can bring. You can move past the sticking point and get her back on track. You might say, for example, "I understand. Perhaps you could clarify for me your specific needs." Then you can adjust your pitch.

Or you might try this: "Perhaps you could point out to me where you see a specific gap between our value proposition and your current objectives." When you encourage the customer to pitch, you gain immediate insight into her goals. You'll be able to identify the black holes in her understanding and adjust them so she can see the light.

Sometimes a buyer will try to put you on the spot by saying, "What are you going to do for me?" or "Tell me how you think this products fits with our plan." Don't get flustered. This is a good sign. Two people who both recognize the value of catching can create more productive give-and-take.

Say you're calling on a customer who owns a small business and has a limited budget. He says, "I don't have the budget for your product." You, the champion salesperson, catch. You nudge the customer to explore solutions with you. "I know that money is a constant issue for you. What are some frustrations or challenges you have with your existing equipment?" Be patient. Remember the difference between the quick score and an effective, enduring relationship. You may want to leave the conversation at a less-than-conclusive juncture, then study the new data and visit the customer again in a few days with a new approach. "If I could show you a way to reduce your overall operating expenses and minimize your future investment in more expensive machines, might you then be interested?"

What customer would say no to that?

When we issue our challenge during workshops, we often observe skeptical, nervous or mystified expressions. One attendee said, "This is way outside the scope of my responsibility." But inevitably people come back from their telephoning with useful insights about their customers. Often they have learned more in one phone call than they had in many years.

Sometimes the challenge is turned back on us. During a seminar with a sales team from Best Foods—at the time the owners of the Skippy, Hellman's and Knorr brands—one participant said he and his colleagues would make a spontaneous phone call if they first had proof it could work. If one of us did it, he said, they would all happily follow suit.

Tom Blake asked for the name of a senior person in the participant's company. "Axel Krause," he said.

The others all chuckled. Tom assumed he was being set up. Krause was the company president—not exactly someone with lots of time on his hands to receive unexpected phone calls. Tom had dealt with the vice president of sales at Best Foods; he had never met Krause.

Tom called the Best Foods switchboard in New Jersey and reached Krause's executive assistant. When she asked who was calling, Tom identified himself and told her, "We're in a seminar with some of your team, and I need to talk to Axel." The assistant said Mr. Krause was extremely busy. Tom said it was very important he speak with Axel. The assistant put Tom on hold, then came back to the phone to say Axel would be right there.

The Best Foods salespeople were giggling with anticipation. When Krause finally came to the phone, his manner was, to say the least, gruff.

"Krause," he said. "What is it you need from me?"

"Axel," replied Tom, "I'm in a meeting right now with a number of your salespeople. We're having a discussion about your business, and some of them don't understand your overall company strategy, in particular how sales and marketing will work together to achieve your goals. I was wondering if I could have your help understanding that."

After a half-hour of listening and gaining invaluable insights that none of the salespeople in the room possessed, Tom, needing to return to the seminar, had to cut Krause off. At the end of the call, Krause asked Tom, "What is it you're teaching my people again?"

"We're teaching them how to ask great questions of their customers."

"That sounds very interesting," said Krause. "Would you send me something on that concept? I'd like to learn more about it."

There is, of course, an obvious problem with catching and never pitching: it can be as non-engaging to a customer as insistent pitching. Championship salespeople strike a productive middle ground in which they control the instinct to pitch and strategically use the skill of catching. The result is a process as free-flowing and vibrant as a father and son throwing a ball back and forth in the yard.

Catching at Home

The concept of catching is critical to business success. But it applies equally to personal relationships. Two of the most gratifying responses we ever received in response to workshops about catching had nothing to do with business.

The first came from a man employed by GBC (General Binding Corporation) in Chicago. At the end of the two-day session, he said, "This concept of catching really transcends business: I've just realized I've spent the past twenty-five years pitching when I get home from work. Tonight, when I get home, I'm going to play a lot more catch."

The second response came from a woman who had participated in one of our training sessions months before. She called one afternoon out of the blue to let us know the effect the session had had on her. Before the training, she was ready to give up on her marriage. She and her husband had agreed to file for divorce. During the catching lesson, she realized that communication issues were affecting their marriage. In failing to catch adequately, she had set up rigid mental walls that prevented her from having constructive exchanges with her husband. In reflex, he had done the same. The result was two people pitching at each other constantly; no one was making the effort to catch.

After the seminar, the woman went home, told her husband what she had learned and encouraged a mutual commitment to catching. Soon the pair had developed ways to appreciate each other's perspectives and break down some of the dysfunctional paradigms they had set up. By embedding the catching instinct, they discovered they had a lot in common.

The lessons learned by these individuals are useful for all of us in our personal lives. Ask yourself if you walk in the door and habitually start pitching about your day. If you do, give catching a try.

PLAYING CATCH

A recent article in the *Journal of Consumer Research* explains a framework called the Persuasion Knowledge Model. Essentially, skepticism immediately takes hold of people when they feel they are being made the target of persuasion attempts—that is, when they feel they are being "sold to." The more suspicious customers are about your motivations, the more skeptical they become toward the claims you make.

For decades, sales research has shown that the most successful salespeople are those best able to communicate meaningfully and effectively. When championship salespeople uphold this mentality, they marry the skills of pitching and catching by opening dialogues, asking appropriate and challenging questions and remembering the information customers provide so they can report to their organizations. Champion salespeople play catch with their customers at every turn.

Let's return to what makes a great sales call. Is it one in which you nailed a pitch, delivered a flawless presentation or sailed uninterrupted through all your PowerPoint slides? No. Is it one in which you asked a single question that got the customer talking for an hour, at which point you left? No. The most valuable, most constructive meeting is one in which there is a game of catch, characterized by a constant flow of give and take, back and forth, questions and answers.

The ability to play catch can be polished. The best salespeople are able to recognize and respond to subtle linguistic signals and small non-verbal cues. They also have an awareness of the customer's tendencies. In the end, only two skills are required to play catch effectively. The first is asking great questions. The second is listening to the answers.

Three Rules for Playing Catch

Recently, a senior executive at a major North American manufacturer shared with us some of his thoughts on playing catch. Despite decades of experience and an ever-expanding skill set, he said he still adheres to three general rules to guide his customer interactions:

1. *Make playing catch with customers a habit.* "It's similar to exercising on a regular basis. If you ingrain it as part of your routine, it starts to become second nature, and the inevitable result is better fitness. Likewise, the more you put yourself in front of customers—and play catch effectively with them—the better your chances for success."

2. *Help customers understand their own strategies.* "It's always interesting having a conversation with customers about their business strategies. Their businesses are very competitive and always changing. By helping them explore new opportunities, you better position yourself to help fill them."

3. *Always ask the question.* "At the conclusion of a recent meeting I had with a top guy at a major grocer generating eight billion a year, I asked what I could do to make our meetings optimally productive. He told me two things:

'First, always tell us the naked truth, even if it will be hard to take. And second, never be afraid to ask us the tough questions.' It reminded me that I still sometimes lapse into thinking customers don't want to play catch. But they always do."

Asking Questions: The Communication Funnel

To understand your customer, you need to get the customer talking. To get the customer talking, you need to know how to initiate a game of catch. To initiate a game of catch, you need to ask the right questions.

Simple, right? Not exactly. Different kinds of questions achieve different purposes. You can use questions to move a customer along the communication funnel, to build insight and find points of connection.

A communication funnel is a tactical guide for customer interactions. At the top of the funnel, questions and statements are informal and non-intrusive. Your goal is to open the discussion by stimulating the customer to talk about current circumstances and business situations. Answers can be as brief or expansive as the customer likes.

The nonthreatening questions build rapport and set the customer at ease. Then the funnel begins to taper toward more sensitive and specific questions. Your aim now shifts—to unearthing information about where the customer is, where it wants to go and how it plans to get there. The more the funnel narrows, the more tact, perceptiveness, strategy and sensitivity you need, and the more valuable the information you gain.

Rapport Building

Purpose Confirmation

Information Gathering

Demonstration of
Understanding

Alignment Seeking

Drilling

Interpretation

© Optimé International Inc.

Figure 7.2: The Communication Funnel

This information will change over time, along with the customer's needs and priorities. In a championship relationship, the communication funnel remains perpetually open at the bottom. The dialogue is never closed; the exchange of insights between salesperson and customer never ends. A championship salesperson is always aware of the possibility that the bottom of one funnel may open to the top of another.

Champion salespeople do not begin customer interactions with complex, probing or sensitive questions. They engage the customer slowly and subtly, guiding the customer through, constantly encouraging dialogue and mutual progress (see Table 7.1).

Inquiring Leaders

When Bill Bratton was sworn in as New York City's police commissioner in 1994, he promised to take on crime in every borough—and to win.[2] Rash though his promise may have seemed, Bratton delivered: he cut the homicide rate by half and reduced serious crime by a third, all in just over two years.

Bratton revealed his main tool for achieving this incredible turnaround: asking questions. He didn't operate from a set of assumptions or seek to confirm what he thought he knew. Instead, he gathered knowledge at ground level—by walking the streets and asking questions of police on their beats. He introduced himself and asked straightforward questions about how things could be improved. By doing so, he identified several new points of leverage and gained invaluable insight into his own city.

Commander D. Michael Abrashoff of the USS *Benfold*—the United States Navy's most modern, most sophisticated warship—doesn't talk like your typical Navy man.[3] When asked what methods he uses to motivate his crew of three hundred, he refers not to war or battle or enemies, but to "aggressive listening."

---

[2] Bratton, W. (1998) *Turnaround: How America's Top Cop Reversed the Crime Epidemic*. Random House, New York.

[3] LaBarre, P. (1999) "Grassroots Leadership: USS *Benfold*," *Fast Company*, April 1999.

Abrashoff believes that the true measure of success is whether his crew members contribute in a meaningful way. He wants to know who they are and where they come from. And he wants them to understand his goals and intentions.

He interviews every new crew member within two days of arrival on board, asking, "What are your goals while you're in the Navy and beyond?" and "What would you change about the *Benfold*?" He implements many of the crew's suggestions. Abrashoff has dramatically increased satisfaction, productivity and staff retention. His example provides a rich lesson for the business world.

Inquiring Cultures

No matter how strategic their questions, inquisitive salespeople cannot do the job alone. To build a full, insightful picture of the customer, the entire organization must reflect a culture of questioning and learning.

The biopharmaceutical firm Ortho Biotech Inc. (OBI) was spun off from its former parent and purchased by a leading multinational manufacturer in 1990. The management board recognized a need to attract the best talent in the biotechnology industry. To that end, they recruited a diverse workforce from various backgrounds. At the same time, the organization faced a major challenge: to get a new product launched quickly, in a new market, within a new organizational structure. OBI's management knew success would result from developing an inquiring culture that could manage diversity effectively.

OBI's leadership team organized three days of meetings for groups of about eighty participants. Groups were mixed by

Table 7.1: Sections of the Communication Funnel

Funnel Section	Nature of Question/ Statement	Examples
Rapport Building	Open-ended	*What do you feel is the best use of our time today? How's your golf game?*
Purpose Confirmation	Obvious, noncontroversial	*My purpose today is to. ... Could you let me know if that accurately represents your understanding as well? You asked to meet today to. ... Does that sound right?*
Information Gathering	Leading	*Could you tell me more? Please go on.*
Demonstration of Understanding	Rephrasing/ Reflecting/ Verifying	*Let me make sure I'm clear on what you're saying. If I understand you properly, you're saying that. ...*
Alignment Seeking	Goal-specific, objective-oriented	*How can we help build your business? What are your main objectives for the coming year?*
Drilling	Sensitive	*What is the company reward program? How exactly does your bonus plan work?*
Interpretation	Inferential, deductive	*Would it be accurate to assume, then, that ...? Does it make sense for me to gather that ...?*

division, race, gender and level. The meeting included a fishbowl exercise in which management board members could collect direct feedback about perceived gaps between OBI's envisioned and actual culture. The board members were permitted only to listen and ask clarifying questions. They were not permitted to explain, defend, correct perceived misinformation or solve problems. Participants formed groups to discuss issues raised during the fishbowl exercise. They made recommendations as to what actions the company should take.

Through these inquiry groups, management created a culture of asking. They put in place a way for employees to communicate issues and concerns; they also imbued employees with the freedom to ask questions. OBI recognized and applied the value of asking questions internally as a way to drive external change.

Half-Funneling

Often, the lower levels of the funnel are intimidating. Some salespeople remain at the safer upper levels. Half-funneling scratches the surface of customer insight but accomplishes little.

Half-funneling is often caused by an inability to dismiss the pitching instinct. Habitual half-funnelers want to get through pleasantries and rapport building so they can begin the pitch. "How's the family?" these people ask. "Great. How's business? The reason I'm here today is to tell you about our new product launch. Shall we dive right in? Feel free to interrupt me with any questions ..."

Championship salespeople recognize that the most valuable customer information lies at the deepest sections of the funnel. They do not stop halfway down. They query and survey, confirm and restate, gently urge, continue to ask the right questions at the right times. They keep the customer in pitching mode and build knowledge as they go.

Resisting the Funnel

The deeper levels of the communication funnel usually require the greatest sensitivity. But champion salespeople remember to pay attention in the upper levels and remain responsive to customer signals. They recognize that sensitivity to the customer sometimes means *not* funneling.

Joe, a talented fast tracker, was preparing to present his company's new product to his top customer, the second largest big-box chain in the country. The product, a groundbreaking over-the-counter medication, was poised to transform its category. Joe's presentation, meticulously developed, captured every nuance and executional detail. Joe had developed a thorough promotional plan that included innovative logistical and financial considerations. He knew his buyer would be impressed.

But when Joe arrived at the buyer's office ready to deliver the thirty-minute presentation, he felt that something was amiss. After pleasantries and some idle conversation, Joe casually asked if anything was on the buyer's mind.

The buyer ignored the question. "What ya got?" he quipped, only half masking his distress. "I'm a busy man!"

Joe's instincts told him to get on with things. All the same, he knew better than to jeopardize the most important product launch in the company's history. He didn't want to present to a distracted buyer. Nor did he want to keep this man from dealing with whatever was on his mind.

Joe looked the buyer in the eye and said, "Look, I know our appointment is short—but is there anything I can do to help?"

The buyer said no and thanked Joe for asking. No sooner had he declined Joe's offer than he began talking. He was having an underground sprinkler system installed, and the contractor had begun to dig up his property. There were large trenches running across his yard. Yesterday it had rained, and he went home from work to find that his kids had maximized the play potential of the muddy trenches, then tromped through the house without removing their clothes or sneakers. The buyer and his wife had recently installed new carpet throughout the house.

After twenty minutes, the buyer fell silent, then said, "Anyway, that's why I'm a bit distracted today."

"I'm really sorry," said Joe, "and I can understand why you'd be feeling less than enthusiastic. Listen, my company is launching the most important product in its history. The truth is I've crafted a launch strategy incorporating your business strategies, financial objectives and logistical imperatives—the whole nine yards. But I don't think I can explain the details in the time we've got left. Do you think we could reschedule for later in the week?"

The buyer glanced at his schedule and saw he was booked solid for the next month.

Joe offered to meet for breakfast, lunch, dinner—any time the buyer could make himself available.

"Joe," the buyer said, "let me see the new item form." Joe handed him the form. After a quick look, the buyer asked, "Can you tell me what the ideal promotional strategy for the new product would look like?"

Joe took five minutes to lay out a top-line vision of success for the new product.

The buyer paused, turned and said, "Consider it done, Joe. And thanks for listening."

If you suppress the instinct to pitch, you can ask questions of the customer. If you ask those questions, you can uncover crucial customer information. But this adjustment is only half of playing catch successfully. Once your questions are asked, the customer starts talking. It's the most critical time in any customer interaction: the time when you're doing nothing but listening.

The Act of Listening

There are two kinds of listening: the kind where the listener hears a string of words coming out of a speaker's mouth, and the kind where the listener actively processes the information contained in those words.

The kind of listening championship salespeople exercise in every customer interaction is *active* listening. The most common misperception regarding listening is that it is a passive act. Listening is, in fact, a dynamic, complex process that requires as much concentration as speaking—or more.

Active listeners employ two important skills. First, they use six principles that encourage customers to share as much information as possible. Then, once they have posed a question, they resist the urge to interrupt or stop listening.

Listening actively means putting aside your own agenda. Most salespeople, asked whether listening to the customer is important, will agree wholeheartedly—yet they fail to realize they are not practicing what they preach.

It's often said the best leaders are great listeners. Champion salespeople ask a question and then focus entirely on the customer. The more you are bound by your own agenda, the more you block yourself from listening and building valuable customer knowledge. When you remain focused on your own message, things the customer says might trigger your "pitch switch." You may start to ignore what she has to say as you look for the next opportunity to say what *you* have to say.

If you keep the dialogue on your message track, not the customer's, you could derail the entire transformational process. A company cannot succeed if the salesperson's knowledge of the customer remains incomplete.

Table 7.2

Active Listening Technique	What It Is	Example
Paraphrasing	Paraphrasing involves restating a message, usually in a more succinct way and using fewer words. By testing your understanding of what you've heard (or thought you heard) the customer say, this technique demonstrates your desire to understand his needs. Successful paraphrasing indicates that you are following the customer's discourse and grasping at least the core of what is being said.	Customer: *My budget is extremely tight.* Salesperson: *You're saying budget is a primary area of concern for you this year.*

Clarifying	Few of us answer questions with instant precision; most of us ramble, take detours and say things like, *What was my point again?* or, *Wait, I just lost what I was trying to say. What was the thing you said before that last thing? No, two things before the last thing.* Clarifying helps bring vague or meandering answers into sharper focus. It demonstrates active listening by untangling unclear interpretation, pushing for additional information, helping the speaker see alternate points of view and identifying exactly what was said.	Customer: *Marketing and IT don't get each other.* Salesperson: *What I think I hear you saying is that your Marketing and IT departments aren't communicating effectively.*
Perception Checking	A salesperson interacting with a customer must be careful not to guide the conversation according to inaccurate assumptions. Champion salespeople subtly request verification of their perceptions along the way. Then they can maintain relevance and bearing, and the dialogue will proceed without hiccups caused by misalignment.	Customer: *This project could be gangbusters, but the players are all over the map.* Salesperson: *Let me see if I've got it straight. You said that you think your current project has plenty of intrinsic upside, but that the working team seems dysfunctional. Is that what you're saying?*

Continued

| Summarizing | As important as checking assumptions along the way is pulling together and organizing the major points discussed and agreed upon. When you summarize, do not insert new ideas. Instead, place key ideas into encapsulating statements. You will solidify understanding between salesperson and customer; you will also create a sense of accomplishment, momentum and closure and help establish a basis for further discussion. | Customer: *We have a real shot at success with this initiative, but everyone has to get on the same page. Right now were working in silos. Also, we need to test the thing before going to market. It's competitive out there. You don't just go to market. You don't plunge in without finding out whether you're going to hit a nerve first.* Salesperson: *It sounds as though you feel the current initiative has great potential, but its success will depend primarily on two things: first, making sure everyone is aligned toward the same goal, and, second, conducting significant preliminary market research.* |

Primary Empathy	When you play a customer's thoughts back to him, you strike a basic but potent chord. Primary empathy is the technique of echoing thoughts back across the table. Use it, and you accomplish a dual purpose: you show you're understanding the customer's experience, and you allow him to evaluate his feelings after he hears them expressed by someone else.	Customer: *There's so much red tape I have to get through to get one decision approved around here.* Salesperson: *You're frustrated by the level of bureaucracy within the organization.*
Advanced Empathy	Primary empathy lets you demonstrate that you understand the customer's experience at a rudimentary level; advanced empathy shows that you understand and can respond to the issues surrounding that experience, and understand its subtleties. Advanced empathy occurs when you reflect the customer's thoughts and statements to him at a deeper level. Advanced empathy often encourages the customer to reveal further insights, pushing the exchange of ideas further along.	Salesperson: *You said that your areas of supervision have broadened into a few different departments. It sounds as though you're also perhaps saying you're being pulled in several directions, which may be proving difficult.* Customer: *Yes—I'm wearing more hats than ever before, and this is not an easy situation to be in. What I really need is for my managers to step up and take charge. I suppose I may not have made that clear to them.*

Barriers to Active Listening

Table 7.3

Barrier	Solution
Thinking about what to say next	Shut off your thoughts and feelings; empty your mind; home in on what the person across from you is saying.
Interrupting/Pouncing	Keep your thoughts on the back burner; file them away until the customer has finished.
Disinterest	Remind yourself that everything the customer is saying has potential value for your relationship.
Drifting/Daydreaming	Tell yourself you might accidentally miss that one nugget that could make all the difference to your business.
Mental Chatter	Envision all competing thoughts or voices in your head being pushed offstage.
Distraction	Maintain focus; give yourself a mental pep talk; imagine turning up the sensitivity knob on your ears.

What Happens When an Entire Country Forgets to Listen?

The act of listening sometimes affects an entire country's global perception. In response to America's flagging image abroad, renowned marketing guru Keith Reinhard—the creative force behind such memorable slogans as "You deserve a break today" and "Like a good neighbor, State Farm is there"—recently formed a nonprofit group called Business for Diplomatic Action. He rounded up 150 marketing and academic heavyweights to help dissect America's "brand" by asking people from other countries what they found disagreeable about the behavior of Americans.

Reinhard's research uncovered a number of characteristics that were serving as roadblocks to successful cross-border relationships. Americans were seen as arrogant, often conveying the attitude that the world revolved around them. They were crass, seldom censoring their speech no matter who was listening. And they were ignorant, displaying little sensitivity or awareness of cultural traditions outside the United States.

One negative trait stood out most prominently: Americans don't *listen*, said those in other parts of the world. They talk constantly and offer opinions endlessly. They rarely adjust the volume knob or encourage dialogue. They always talk and hardly ever listen, so they never learn about people with whom they are trying to build relationships.

Reinhard's group prepared booklets and other helpful documents recommending how Americans can behave when they travel abroad. Recommended change number one: stop talking and start listening.

Questions for Playing Catch

Just as great actors make acting look easy, those who have mastered the game of catch execute it with such subtlety and ease that their partners often don't know a game is occurring. The dexterity needed for successful catching does not necessarily come easily. You must be sensitive to the shifting rhythms of conversation. You must cultivate the ability to know when to talk and when to listen. Here are open-ended questions you can use to get a customer talking.

- What are the key elements of your business plan this year?

- What are the operating strategies that will drive your day-to-day business?

- What are your key deliverables/priorities?

- What are the biggest issues you are facing/hurdles you anticipate having to overcome?

- What measurement criteria are you using to make decisions about your business operations?

- Who else should we be talking to in your company regarding potential synergies?

- How can we better help you add value?

- As a supplier/potential supplier, what changes within your systems, processes or overall structure should we be aware of?

- How might we adjust our business model for competitive advantage with you?

- How can we better capitalize on opportunities with your company?

Pausing for Effect

Any successful handyman knows that impulsiveness can hinder success. Every house project—from hanging a picture to building a deck—has a better chance of success when you pause to assess, plan, react or improvise.

Pausing is also valuable when you are playing catch. Champion sellers employ two related skills to derive optimal benefit from games of catch with their customers. First, they suppress the instinct to pitch by asking strategic questions instead. Second, they wait for answers.

Pausing is one of the most effective and under-utilized communication tools in personal interaction. It's also more difficult in practice than in theory. Sometimes you ask a question and the customer does not respond instantly. You might think, *What if the customer didn't understand the question? What if it didn't make sense in the first place? What if I already asked it five minutes ago?*

More often than not, the customer is thinking about how to answer. If you let the pause continue, you encourage the customer to answer in detail, continue a previous thought or provide new information. If you fill the pause, you close off the question.

When you feel yourself itching to fill a pause, practice these techniques:

- Say "Shh" to yourself (in your head—not out loud).
- Count to ten. (You will probably get a response from the customer before you get to ten.)
- Bite your tongue (but keep your lips closed).

OUTCOMES OF PLAYING CATCH

Watch two people tossing a baseball back and forth—father and son, brother and sister, a pair of friends. Watch them anywhere— in the backyard, on the street or during recess at school. Watch their faces as the game heats up and they encourage each other to throw with a little extra mustard.

Observe them in the act of throwing. Notice their focus and intensity. Watch them computing trajectory, analyzing where the target is and how to meet it. Then, as they catch, notice a different sensation. As ball meets leather, issuing its loud, satisfying *WHAP!*, both parties experience an instant of powerful connection. They throw with greater gusto, seeking to replicate that moment as often as possible. Their eyes gleam brightly and their grins expand. They fall into a shared rhythm, the tempo of the game like a metronome.

There is a shared rhythm in a game of catch between a champion salesperson and a customer. Neither tries to overpower the other; both forget who is pitching and who is catching during the information exchange and reciprocal discovery.

When you use the two transformational skills basic to playing catch—asking great questions and listening actively to the answers—you initiate and guide the game. You are conscious of tempo; you pitch when necessary, catch constantly. Sometimes the customer's throws are imprecise, and you must stretch, bend or leap to snare the ball. Sometimes you have to feel each other out before you achieve a mutual cadence. Sometimes the customer holds the ball, uncertain how to throw it back, and you must deliver subtle encouragement through tactical inquiry.

With patience, purpose and strategic application of a catching approach, you can establish a common pulse with the customer. The give-and-take generates relevant information that can be used for further discussion. The give-and-take can also lead to a vigorous game of catch that may be erratic in places yet still bring to light specific insights your sales organization can build on. At its peak, the back-and-forth becomes one rhythm.

Expanding the Game

As you play catch with the customer, you learn about synergies being leveraged within the organization and fissures threatening it; about which different stakeholders are attempting to address similar problems; about issues facing different people in different roles and with different levels of influence or authority. A single game of catch might reveal four or five new areas to examine, something a pitch can never do.

Champion salespeople often find themselves with new people at the customer organization to call on. The implication for business is clear. A car with four tires on the road has better traction than a car with only one; climbing a rope using two hands and two feet is vastly easier than doing it with one hand; and a fly with four feet on a spider's web is going to have a much harder time getting away than a fly who has made only a single tentative step.

Playing catch with different people at various levels of the organization creates competitive advantage and leads to a higher degree of interdependency. It engenders a more synthesized understanding of the customer's needs and produces multiple touchpoints throughout the customer organization. You can increase account penetration, boost call frequency and enhance value across functions.

With a larger piece of business, it is more important to play catch with different people at the customer organization. The fewer robust touchpoints you have, the more tenuous your grip on the project. By playing catch with people throughout the customer company, your grip is reinforced.

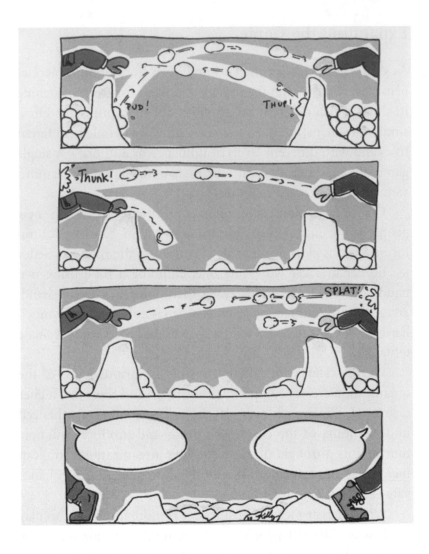

When two parties pitch constantly at each other, the most common result is that both come away having accomplished nothing at all.

Figure 7.3: Pitcher vs. Pitcher

The meeting with her buyer successfully concluded, Barb, the customer sales leader, conducts one of her habitual walks through the customer offices, greeting people she knows, introducing herself to others. Her walks are not part of a conscious strategy—she simply loves to talk to people. She suspects this is the reason she was drawn to sales.

When she returns to her office, her boss remarks on how many people she knows at the customer organization. I suppose that's true, Barb thinks, *though I never really thought about it before.*

The boss says she is on to something and instructs her to do two things: schedule meetings with all the people she knows at that customer organization to find out their particular needs, and share her walk-around strategy with her co-workers. When word gets out and she is asked about her walks, Barb tells everyone who asks, "I just talk to people. I ask them questions—about how their business is doing, about what could be done better, about what specific obstacles they face. And when a solution occurs to me that we can offer, I bring it up."

Other people in the sales organization begin to apply the method, and soon the company has increased its fingertip hold on the customer to a relationship with multiple points and numerous initiatives. In retrospect, everyone realizes that the way to connect with the customer is to do what Barb has always done—play catch with people in different roles, at different levels. By taking the most natural behavior in the world—talking to others—and making it a formal part of customer strategy, the organization has left its competitors wondering what it is suddenly doing so right.

These days, every company under the sun is searching for ways to create customer loyalty. Having multiple touchpoints between customer and supplier builds true sticking power and makes it difficult for a customer to disengage. It's a lot easier to sever a relationship with a supplier whose structure is traditional—or transactional—than one whose structure is based on customer-centric—or championship—principles. The broader mindset and higher level of thinking demanded by championship selling results in a greater return on investment; a wider array of products will be purchased by the customer, and loyalty will increase by leaps and bounds.

Companies today are investing millions in loyalty programs and customer incentive bundles in the hopes of acquiring and retaining customers. Meanwhile, astute organizations are cementing loyalty by establishing true championship orientations. Their competitive advantage proves critical when customers need to assess budgets and decide where their dollars should be invested. If you've been working with one or two contacts on a single project with a certain customer, your level of interdependency is low and your expendability is high. If you regularly call on people throughout the company, your level of interdependency becomes high, which makes you a near-indispensable supplier. You are someone who creates value for your company by regularly playing catch, gaining continuous insights and providing well-informed solutions.

Your rewards will include increased call frequency, higher customer engagement and enhanced relationship diversity. In the new world of selling, people at the top of the heap focus on bringing together their company and the entire customer organization.

Imagine the transformation achieved when two organizations are brought together. Envision yourself walking through your customer's office, the orchestrator of company resources, bringing and creating value for both your company and your customer's. You no longer know only one buyer and a smattering of other people; you know people across all levels and functions. Business growth and sales will follow.

Salespeople and suppliers in every industry struggle to increase account penetration. Often they try to achieve the goal using every method but the most fruitful: talking to the customer. No formula, if it does not include playing catch, will lead to deeper account penetration or optimized customer relationships. The best way to ascertain your customer's situation is to ask—even if you've asked before—and to keep asking. An even better way is to ask other people, as well.

---

10 Golden Rules for Playing Catch

1. Ask open-ended questions first, and often.

2. Ask sensitive questions only after open communication has been established and you are confident in the relationship.

3. Ask the same question of different people, at multiple levels, in different departments, to gain perspective.

4. Ask a similar question of the customer at least once every quarter.

5. Ask new questions.

Continued

6. Ask variations on old questions to gain new insights.

7. Ask questions that relate to the customer's business plan.

8. Ask questions explicitly designed to encourage business value for the customer.

9. Ask the questions nobody else asks.

10. Ask what not to ask.

CONTINUING THE CLIMB

Adopting a championship perspective—the first level of the Performance Pyramid—enables you to understand your own biases, ideals and mental paradigms and to approach your customers with confidence, honesty and a genuine interest in reciprocal advantage. With this perspective in place, you come naturally to replace pitching with playing catch. Playing catch effectively, with as many members of the other team as possible, allows you to gather precious raw information about the customer's needs and goals and enables you to reach the decisive third level of the Performance Pyramid: developing a plan for strategic customer management.

10 QUESTIONS FOR REFLECTION: PLAYING CATCH

- Do I usually go into a customer call thinking, *Here's what my products can do for you*? Or do I go in aiming to understand the customer's agenda and provide pertinent solutions?

- Am I more in control when pitching or catching?

- In my last customer call, how much time did I spend pitching versus catching?

- Do I always try to pitch all the material I've got with me?

- Do I ask strategic questions?

- Do I listen actively to the answers and continue to explore them?

- Do I attempt to drill down through the communication funnel—and continue to do so over time?

- Am I aware of tools such as paraphrasing, clarifying and perception checking?

- Do I initiate games of catch with stakeholders at different levels of the customer organization? If not, what is preventing me from doing so?

- How do I define a great customer call? Is it one in which I deliver a great pitch, making the customer understand everything about me? Or is it one in which I have a great game of catch that lets me understand everything about the customer?

CHAPTER 8

Preparation: Developing a Plan for Strategic Customer Management

The will to win is important, but the will to prepare is vital.

—Joe Paterno

Championship salespeople know how to play catch. They maintain a customer-centric approach, subtly guide conversations with the right combination of great questions and active listening, and capably drill deep into the communication funnel to draw out crucial information.

The process of playing catch is only the preliminary step in a broader process that creates tremendous value for the customer.

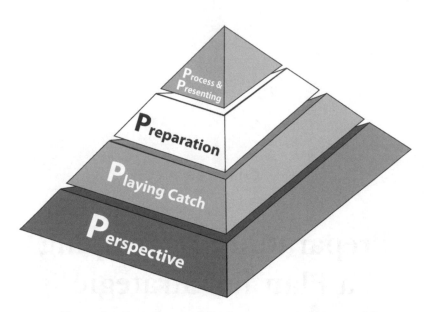

Figure 8.1: Performance Pyramid Featuring Preparation

The information you derive from a great game of catch, though essential, is unprocessed. An enormous amount of work—at multiple levels, by many individuals, in a highly coordinated manner—is required to produce the bottle of oil or package of sugar we buy in the store. People who take that bottle or package from the shelf and add it to their cart don't think of it as the end product in an intricate process. They don't envision the complex machinery that has gone into producing it. They don't consider the degree of combined thinking, analysis and effort that has enabled the right product to be offered to them at just the time they need it.

The culmination of a strategic customer management plan may be observed when the salesperson delivers a specific, well-considered, relevant solution, but before that, a sophisticated process is carried out behind the scenes. The importance of this process is highlighted by a recent comment from Warren Buffett. Asked by *Fortune* to relate the best piece of knowledge he'd ever received in business, he said, "You're right not because others agree with you but because your facts are right."

Through playing catch, the champion salesperson gathers deep, rich information about the customer's targets and aspirations, the consumer, the competition, and, of course, his own company. In the background, the championship sales organization stands poised to transform that information into a specific strategic customer management plan for success. The championship salesperson and the championship organizational culture become a collective force far greater than the sum of their individual parts.

THE NEW WORLD

The field of selling has undergone myriad changes in recent years. Warp-speed technology and the availability of data at increasingly granular levels have radically altered the selling process and the expectations of those who buy. Gone forever is the time when buyers and sellers met individually, when products either met the customer's needs or didn't, when a salesperson's primary goal was to fill call quotas.

Customers today are a sophisticated lot. What's more, their organizations have developed into multilayered operations with complex organizational structures, numerous interrelated objectives and specific financial criteria against which buyers, sellers and partners are measured. Yet many salespeople continue to deal with a single touchpoint: the same buyer they've been dealing with for as long as they've been calling on the customer. As a result, their understanding of the customer's requirements is sliding backward.

Some salespeople and their organizations understand that the sales function needs to become more sophisticated to be successful. As customers become bigger and more complex, organizations must be able to create more versatile solutions, and their salespeople must become orchestrators of company resources to deliver value propositions that hit the customer's bullseye. They must become forward-thinking advisers who conceive, refine and deliver a specific business plan to fit the customer's distinctive requirements.

The new-age salesperson is no longer just a relationship builder. Relationship building is now a given. Today's champion maintains a larger view that combines relationship management and business value. The champion hits at a higher level than the transactional salesperson, who is merely looking to close a deal, or the relationship manager, whose focus on personal selling sometimes comes at the expense of a substantial business proposition.

Today's championship salesperson perceives sales as an ongoing process rather than a series of discrete events captured within individual transactions. This perception impels champions to think and act like customer general managers. All this is a far cry from the "ship the goods" focus of the past.

The more business evolves and accelerates, the clearer this truth becomes. As a customer general manager, the championship salesperson helps other people in the organization and approaches issues with a big-picture, long-term approach. The champion realizes that asking for help within the company is a sign of strength. The champion adopts a strategic approach to harness the value of the entire organization to meet the customer's agenda. The champion is equally quick to hold the customer's hand or administer a gentle nudge depending on which is required. And the champion's knowledge of what the customer needs is never more than a half a step behind the customer's.

The Value of the Blank Page

As former president of global customer business development for Procter & Gamble, recently retired Tom Muccio oversaw some of the most important supplier-customer relationships in the business world. Tom was one of the first to pioneer the concept of multifunctional customer teams; he encouraged all his salespeople to think like general managers of their customer relationships. This meant implementing measurement tools for success and jointly developed scorecards; it was important for both sides to know exactly how scores would be kept and what success would look like.

It also meant training members of the sales organization to think strategically about business growth and develop business plans alongside their customers. To do this would require the ability to converse with top customer executives, making a brand new skill set—and mindset—prerequisites for success.

Tom would direct his multifunctional, multi-resource teams to think about developing a document similar in scope and sophistication to a company's cross-functional strategic plan that would outline projects, timelines and responsibilities, and to determine the customer's specific goals and strategies before attempting to sell them anything. His goal was to establish solid customer teams and the company infrastructure to support them. Some of these multifunctional customer teams became industry benchmarks.

We asked Tom about the techniques that allowed him to create a more strategic customer approach. Tom provided a classic less-is-more answer. "When I first met with the people from Wal-Mart, I just went in with a blank pad and asked as many questions as I could. Half the time I didn't even understand what they were talking about. But that step—going in seeking to learn about the customer instead of pushing the company agenda—was the first in becoming a true customer general manager. Carrying that same attitude into every interaction set the tone for the entire relationship to follow."

Soft-spoken, easygoing and more disposed to listen than to talk—in many ways, the very antithesis of the sales executive stereotype—Richard Touzalin was for many years one of the top salespeople at Pfizer, the pharmaceutical and consumer product goods giant. Conversations with Richard's superiors and customers reveal the reasons for his success: a management perspective inside-out and outside-in. Richard was driven not by slickness, power or manipulation but by his customer management perspective—in-depth knowledge of his company's offerings on one end and his customer's needs on the other. Richard epitomizes the true championship salesperson. Both his company and his customers say he knows them as well as anyone possibly could.

Richard's approach points the way to the championship salesperson of tomorrow: insightful, understanding, empathetic, sensitive. People who adopt the championship model will strengthen their competitive footing to find new opportunities, new horizons and new definitions of success.

THE VIRTUOUS KNOWLEDGE CYCLE

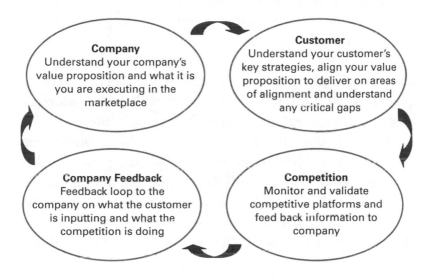

Company
Understand your company's value proposition and what it is you are executing in the marketplace

Customer
Understand your customer's key strategies, align your value proposition to deliver on areas of alignment and understand any critical gaps

Company Feedback
Feedback loop to the company on what the customer is inputting and what the competition is doing

Competition
Monitor and validate competitive platforms and feed back information to company

Figure 8.2: Virtuous Knowledge Cycle

Championship salespeople and their organizations maintain a continuous loop of knowledge sharing among salesperson, sales organization and customer. This loop allows them to deliver tightly focused, directly aligned solutions. We call this loop the Virtuous Knowledge Cycle.

The Virtuous Knowledge Cycle begins when the championship salesperson develops an intricate knowledge of her company's value proposition. By challenging herself to understand her products and services, the championship salesperson sets the cycle in motion.

Once she has mastered knowledge of her company's product or service, she proceeds to the next part of the Virtuous Knowledge Cycle: playing catch with the customer. Her goal is to learn about the customer's situation, to obtain as much information as the customer is willing to give, to discuss general goals as well as drill down into specific objectives and intended outcomes. As she listens and absorbs, she is thinking about how the customer's goals might align with the company value proposition.

Before feeding the information into the championship organization waiting to process it, the salesperson makes a careful study of the competition. She combines what she learned from the customer with what she has learned about the competition, then begins to think about solutions that will meet the customer's needs and differentiate her efforts from the efforts of her competitors.

Armed with critical information about the customer's needs and goals and the activities of the competition, the championship salesperson returns to the company to begin marshalling resources to fulfill the customer objective. By playing catch, she has determined what the customer wants to achieve; by paying attention, she has evaluated the competition's efforts. Now, supported by an outward-facing company culture, she uses her company's resources to assemble a unique solution.

In the championship organization, the necessary resources are present and oriented directly toward the customer. The give-and-take between sales and all other functions may at first seem conscious and deliberate, but over time it becomes automatic. The interaction stimulates a continual loop of customer-oriented knowledge building, refinement of the company's value proposition and increased focus in delivery.

If the salesperson spends her time with the customer pitching instead of catching, the virtuous cycle stalls. If she catches successfully but brings the acquired knowledge to a company whose resources are not set up to help develop a strategic customer management plan, the virtuous cycle stalls. If she fails to investigate the solutions offered by her competitors, she is ignoring a potentially large blind spot. But the combination of customer-oriented salesperson and customer-centric organization, with a dash of insight into the competition, enables the cycle to continue. The crafting of the customer solution is an exercise completed by multiple helping hands.

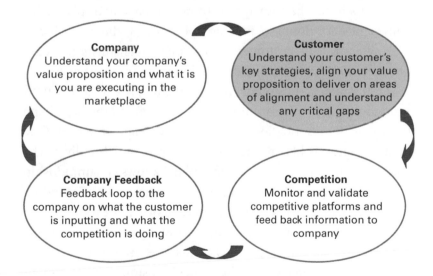

Figure 8.3: Virtuous Knowledge Cycle Featuring the Strategic Customer Management Plan

APPROACHING THE STRATEGIC CUSTOMER MANAGEMENT PLAN

When the championship salesperson brings into his organization the sensitive mixture of its own value proposition, the customer's needs and information about the competition, the company undertakes the most important step in the Virtuous Knowledge Cycle: mapping all the knowledge against a framework we call the strategic customer management plan. This tool is invaluable for developing a thorough, evolving picture of the customer and understanding how the customer thinks, acts and operates. The essential goal of the championship salesperson is to get inside the customer's head; the strategic customer management plan is his main vehicle for doing so. Forcing upon oneself the discipline of creating a strategic customer management plan turns raw data into precious insight, basic information into strategic wisdom.

The strategic customer management plan will be used throughout the organization. It is an encyclopedic, living document, the foundation for an effective plan of action. One might imagine it like an architectural draft of a building. The strategic customer management plan allows championship performers to penetrate the surface and gain an understanding of a customer's inner workings. There is one critical difference, however, between an architectural drawing and the strategic customer management plan: whereas the architect is always seeking a precise, final vision, the strategic customer management plan is always changing.

Your customers are making decisions that affect your business every day. The more knowledgeable you can be about what they want to accomplish, the more you can positively influence their decisions. Developing a strategic customer management plan allows you to determine who does what and who knows what inside the customer's organization, how things get done, who is a rising (or falling) star, what the president is working on, what the manager is concerned about and what the organization's biggest issues are. All these pieces of information, when gathered, lead to more sustainable partnerships.

When an individual salesperson tells us he or she has been calling on a customer for years and knows everything there is to know about that customer, we're skeptical. Those who say they know the most typically know the least. We call this the KIA (Know It All) syndrome. It represents the opposite of the instinct for generating strategic customer management plans. The idea that you know everything about someone because you've interacted with them for a long time is fundamentally flawed.

Salespeople affected by KIA often sense they don't, in fact, know it all, but don't want to confirm this suspicion. So they don't ask questions; they cruise on the same assumptions week after week, month after month, year after year.

The nature of your interaction with the customer determines whether your knowledge of the customer stagnates or evolves. All organizations change over time, driving the need for strategic customer management plans. What you knew about a company last year, last month or last week means nothing if you don't know that customer's situation today.

Here's a test to gauge your general level of customer understanding and penetration.

- What are your buyer's top five performance metrics this year?

- What has changed from the previous year?

- What are the performance metrics of your buyer's boss?

- What are the three most important strategies your customer is focused against?

- How do the people you call on integrate their performance metrics into the corporate strategy?

- How do regional offices influence decisions made at head office? Who are the most influential players in the regional offices? When was the last time you spent constructive time with them?

- Who are the key business influencers outside procurement? In what ways are they your allies?

If you can answer these questions, strategic customer management plans, or something like them, are probably already part of your working repertoire. If you find the answers hard to come by, you might be in the same boat as an account manager we dealt with recently.

The account manager—let's call him Al—had been calling on the headquarters of a major retailer for fifteen years and was lauded as one of the most successful salespeople in the company. It wasn't unusual for Al's individual growth and success rates to outpace those of the sales organization. In the most recent fiscal year, the company had achieved a five-percent overall increase, but Al's business had grown by seven percent. He was acknowledged as a top salesperson who knew his customers extremely well.

During a company-wide shuffle, Al was moved to another account. Another fifteen-year veteran, Ed, was brought in to replace him. Ed had no experience in sales; he had spent time in other departments and knew plenty about his company's value proposition, but was a rookie when it came to selling.

To illustrate the power of championship selling and playing catch, we like to ask our clients how they imagine Ed did, compared to Al. The almost universal assumption is that Ed probably had difficulty meeting Al's performance. In fact, the sales rookie doubled the business.

How did he do it? By venturing into the relationship with no assumptions about what the customer needed or valued. In other words, he began the relationship afresh. He spent time with the customer asking plenty of questions and creating a preliminary map of its objectives, then compared these to his company's value proposition. Al had achieved sales increases, but he had been working on cruise control. He had likely stopped asking questions of the customer years earlier. He assumed that the customer would buy enough to keep everyone happy. Ed, on the other hand, went in with a blank slate and asked the customer plenty of questions. His tactic drove business off the charts. The lesson? Championship salespeople operate always on the logical assumption of constant flux; they make it their business to continually update the strategic customer management plan and its particular components. They are always intimately familiar with points of entry, areas of sensitivity within the overall structure and ways they might help their company become more valuable.

The KIA syndrome can also strike at the organizational level.

The senior executives at a top manufacturing company are trying to determine a sales and marketing

approach that will boost business with the organization's
customers. It's clear the current approach has lost any
effect it might once have had. They approach some
objective experts for assistance. The experts know
little about the manufacturing industry but visit the
company's largest global customers.

They attempt to form an initial strategic customer
management plan: they ask questions of each customer
about the relationship with the manufacturing company
and how that company might better position its offering
to fulfill their needs.

The customers mention that the sessions are eye-
opening and valuable. They also say it's the first time
the company has asked what the customers want.
Some people say when the manufacturers' sales
leaders come calling, they pitch relentlessly and seldom
ask about the customer's goals. The company doesn't
understand its customers' needs. By going in with a
blank strategic customer management plan and trying
to populate it, the experts, with no particular wisdom or
insight into the industry, have made the customers feel
that the company is finally starting to get it.

The Strategic Customer Management Roadmap

The development of a strategic customer management plan
requires an appreciation of business strategy and a tactical mindset
coupled with a commitment to thorough implementation.
Creation of a strategic customer management plan involves ten
steps. The first four focus on strategy, the final six on execution.
The rationale of the strategic customer management plan

runs counter to the traditional (transactional) inclination of salespeople. For them, execution is often the sole focus.

The strategic customer management plan positions salespeople as representatives of a larger team that shares a collective focus on the customer. The salespeople are encouraged to study the customer first, then to intelligently engage the customer at levels of increasing depth, to understand its needs, to study further and, finally, to come back with a precise solution.

An individual fact, when placed under the microscope of the strategic customer management plan, can suddenly reveal important information about the customer's agenda. Unrelated facts that seem to be disparate pieces of different puzzles suddenly coalesce, illuminating points of alignment previously undetected. These discoveries can mean countless dollars earned, and ultimately they can make the difference between modest improvements and breakthrough customer solutions.

Following are the ten steps of building a strategic customer management plan.

STEP 1

Objective: Understand your company's qualitative priorities and quantitative goals.

Why It's Crucial: Recording the opportunities you're trying to create for a particular customer can help you understand what you're trying to achieve overall as a company. When salespeople don't understand their company's goals or strategies, they are liable to make promises or commitments the company can't deliver on.

STEP 2

Objective: Articulate the customer's strategies, priorities, current situation and value proposition going forward.

Why It's Crucial: The difference between assumption and fact can make or break your relationship with a customer. When you feed the knowledge you gained playing catch into the strategic customer management plan, you clarify, in the customer's language and according to its sensibilities, its needs— independent of any assumptions you may have. The better you can articulate what the customer wants, the stronger your ability to work strategically with them.

STEP 3

Objective: Find points of linkage between your goals and priorities and those of the customer.

Why It's Crucial: Developing the strategic customer management plan is useless if steps one and two are not combined—that is, if a company simply moves forward on the customer agenda without thinking about how that agenda interacts with its own value proposition. *Strategic alignment* and *basic partnership* are different concepts. Basic partnership involves doing exactly what the customer wants and could require you to forfeit your company's strategy. Strategic alignment means finding common ground between your goals and the goals of the customer. Central to step three is the idea that there will be areas of alignment and nonalignment. Zero in on the areas of alignment and highlight them to the customer. Don't expend time and energy trying to squeeze out extra revenue from the customer based on your own needs. Instead, take some time to stand in the customer's shoes; new options will open up.

STEP 4

Objective: Define the agenda for success and outline how you will deliver mutual achievement over a defined period.

Why It's Crucial: Numerous general points of alignment may reveal themselves during creation of the strategic customer management plan; boiling these down to two or three main objectives can help focus the team.

STEP 5

Objective: Identify champions on both sides.

Why It's Crucial: The most compelling plan will not work unless both suppliers and customers push it along. Find people in the customer's company who can move the agenda forward. Ask the same question of your own company. Look at every level of both organizations—key championship teams often contain unlikely people.

Executing at the Three Levels of Customer Influence

Critical to successful championship selling is the development of a cohesive, well-considered business strategy tailored to the customer's needs, goals and particular circumstances. Equally important is to execute this strategy properly by engaging different people at various levels of the customer organization.

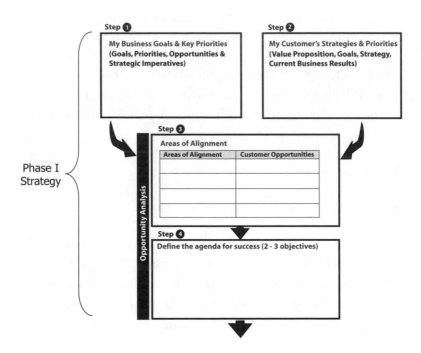

Figure 8.4: The Strategic Customer Management Plan

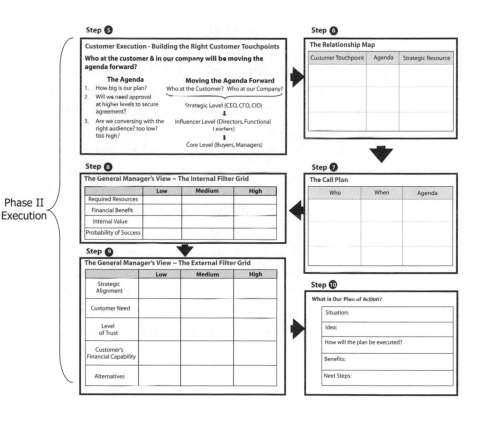

Phase II Execution

Step ❺

Customer Execution - Building the Right Customer Touchpoints

Who at the customer & in our company will be moving the agenda forward?

The Agenda
1. How big is our plan?
2. Will we need approval at higher levels to secure agreement?
3. Are we conversing with the right audience? too low? too high?

Moving the Agenda Forward
Who at the Customer? Who at our Company?

Strategic Level (CEO, CFO, CIO)
↓
Influencer Level (Directors, Functional Leaders)
↓
Core Level (Buyers, Managers)

Step ❻

The Relationship Map

Customer Touchpoint	Agenda	Strategic Resource

Step ❼

The Call Plan

Who	When	Agenda

Step ❽

The General Manager's View ~ The Internal Filter Grid

	Low	Medium	High
Required Resources			
Financial Benefit			
Internal Value			
Probability of Success			

Step ❾

The General Manager's View ~ The External Filter Grid

	Low	Medium	High
Strategic Alignment			
Customer Need			
Level of Trust			
Customer's Financial Capability			
Alternatives			

Step ❿

What is Our Plan of Action?

Situation:
Idea:
How will the plan be executed?
Benefits:
Next Steps:

Table 8.1 is a guide to the three key levels of organizational decision makers and the circumstances in which they should be approached.

Most of the organizations we work with on strategic customer management are deeply connected at the core level but deficient at the influencer and strategic levels. A crucial part of the strategic customer management plan is to list all those involved on the customer side—including significant players at all three levels—and determine the precise degree to which they will potentially affect the mutual agenda for success going forward. Once this exercise is completed, it is crucial to match the size and nature of your proposed solution to the individual at the appropriate level. For example, taking high-level strategic plans to those at the core touchpoint level is a recipe for rejection, since people at this level are usually in touch with several suppliers and desire easy, quick solutions to the issues on their plate. On the flipside, approaching a chief officer to explain a granular, tactical, ground-level product solution is equally imprudent. Matching solution to level of influence at the customer organization is vital, enabling the championship salesperson to continue moving forward through the strategic customer management plan.

STEP 6

Objective: Create the relationship map.

Why It's Crucial: Identifying who is involved in the overall project is a basic step; identifying specific customer touchpoints to hit and how to hit each one takes your effort to the next level.

Table 8.1

	Characteristics	Typical Roles	Appropriate When ...
Core Level	• Organizational "doers" • Key to basic functioning of organization	• Buyer • Procurement Manager • Operations Manager • Warehouse Manager	• Decision to be made is relatively small, often requiring a simple yes or no response (e.g., approval of a product change)
Influencer Level	• Key change agents within context of company's day-to-day operations • Extensive responsibility but relatively limited decision-making authority	• Director • Functional Leader • Analyst (IT, Logistics, Finance) • Senior Vice President	• Change to be proposed is in an operational context (e.g., large purchase decision not affecting company's overall strategic direction but requiring buy-in at various levels)
Strategic Level	• Key decision makers for significant change affecting short-term or long-term direction of company	• CEO • CFO • CIO	• Proposal involves significant change for the customer organization and agenda for success is broad in scope, requiring buy-in at multiple levels (e.g., adopting new company-wide technology)

STEP 7

Objective: Devise the call plan.

Why It's Crucial: Constructing the broad agenda for success over a defined period takes care of one essential goal. Laying out the details—the people you need to see, when to see them and what to discuss—takes care of the other.

STEP 8

Objective: Put the plan through an internal filter.

Why It's Crucial: Confirming that the plan makes sense within your company's goals—the goals you ingrained in step one—is an effective way to be sure you're on the right track. Address four critical questions: What are the required resources? What is the financial benefit? What is the internal value? What is the probability of success?

STEP 9

Objective: Put the plan through an external filter.

Why It's Crucial: When you confirm that your plan fits the goals of the customer, you also determine the level of engagement the customer is likely to demonstrate. Within the external filter you must look at five specific factors: 1) strategic alignment between the customer's current configuration and the proposed agenda and the extent to which the customer's current systems and policies will need to be modified so the agenda can be realized; 2) whether the customer need for the proposed agenda is high, medium or low; 3) the level of trust and credibility within the customer relationship; 4) the customer's financial capability and whether its level of willing investment matches the agenda for success; and 5) whether an alternative plan exists; in other words, if the customer doesn't go with your offering, can they do it themselves? Can a competitor?

STEP 10

Objective: Present the plan.

Why It's Crucial: Development of the strategic customer management plan culminates when you present the plan to the customer. No amount of research or examination is useful unless the plan is delivered in the right way, at the right time, by the right people to the right people.

Strategic Customer Management in Action

A customer general manager at a global Fortune 500 player was told by the company's senior executives that the growth target for his top customer had been increased from three percent to twelve for the coming year. Paul, the GM, wasn't sure how he was going to deliver. Good relationship management and a strong effort from the sales organization had already made his customer number one with the company—but to achieve this kind of leap in a single year? That was tantamount to catching lightning in a bottle. His confidence dipped when his team's intense scrutiny of the company's brands revealed only marginal opportunities for improvement.

Then Paul realized something. He'd been so focused on his own agenda, he had neglected to look at the customer's. He asked his team members to meet and play catch with people at various levels of the customer's organization. He included several vice presidents, directors and buyers; each would likely provide different points of view, thereby giving a broader aggregate perspective. This multilevel strategic customer interaction revealed that the customer's agenda was focused squarely on increasing profitability, centralizing operations and standardizing merchandising nationally. This was not promising news for Paul, since the customer's goal hardly aligned with his company's.

Paul's team had been delivering high volume but low profit margin. Among twenty suppliers, they ranked at the bottom. They were operating in a decentralized fashion, delivering most of their strongest results regionally. Matching up with the customer's agenda seemed an overwhelming challenge—until the entire team agreed on a shift in mindset. They would change their key measure from volume to profit.

A quick profit analysis of the one hundred brands Paul's team regularly sold to the customer revealed some illuminating facts. More than half the brands they were selling delivered profit margins equal to or greater than the targets the customer had set out. But the customer had inadvertently de-emphasized these brands in deference to big brands with low profit margins.

The team devised a two-pronged solution to satisfy the customer's agenda. First, they set up a double-the-volume-double-the-profit program; then they set up a national strategy to centralize the customer's merchandising effort.

Both strategies were embraced by the customer as breakthrough ideas for shifting its business model. Toward the end of the process, Paul's team discovered that government legislation would soon require the customer to discontinue the sale of tobacco products in a large number of its retail outlets. The legislation would cause a revenue shortfall of $100 million. But the legislation proved serendipitous—it conferred tremendous leverage for selling the double-the-volume-double-the-profit plan.

The results of the new plan were staggering. When other companies eventually received the news about the new tobacco legislation, they discovered they'd been beaten to the punch. As a result of proactively driving the strategic customer management plan, Paul's company's products had already been ordered to fill the tobacco void. By focusing the company's brands on the customer's objectives, Paul and his team had done more than meet expectations; they had hit the ball clear out of the park.

The exercise of developing a strategic customer management plan forces a championship discipline that incorporates strategy into the overall customer approach. While building the plan, you have to step back and look at your customer's goals in relation to your own value proposition. As a salesperson, you have played catch with key people in the customer organization and assembled precious information about its ambitions. You have fed that knowledge into your organization; your company's resources are structured in a customer-oriented way. Together, the individual piston (the salesperson) and the overall engine (the organization) have arrived at a forceful, winning solution, which will be communicated to the customer. Imagine a cartoon in which some object is shoved into one end of a large, chugging contraption to be spat out the other end as a more developed, more refined, more sophisticated version of itself. In this case, the company's own value proposition, raw customer knowledge and competitor information are the ingredients fed into the front end, and the aligned solution is what comes out the other side.

Having created the strategic customer management plan, the championship salesperson is ready to head back to the customer with specific ideas for connecting its needs with the company's products or services. The salesperson is justifiably confident in the plan, and the customer is understandably receptive to it, since it is based on thorough knowledge of both ends of the interaction and results from a conscientious examination of points of alignment between company offering and customer objectives.

As the relationship between salesperson and customer—actually the relationship between company and customer, with the salesperson as orchestrator—develops and expands, the Virtuous Knowledge Cycle continues. The salesperson stays fully abreast of his company's changing products, continues to play catch frequently with the customer to keep his finger on the pulse of its ongoing needs, regularly assesses the efforts of the competition and constantly reports the information to the company, whose resources are positioned for continuous development of the strategic customer management plan. The company can fulfill the customer's needs. And that makes for a happy customer.

One of our favorite examples of successful strategic customer management involved a leading retailer that wanted to increase profitability in the baby-care category. Initial research showed that the company's baby formula was performing poorly—so poorly, in fact, that it was responsible for a significant profit shortfall. There seemed to be only one logical solution: cut the loss and discontinue the product.

This company, experienced and wise, asked the marketing function to find points of high-sensitivity alignment between its products and customers' buying patterns. The marketing function conducted a thorough strategic customer management exercise to uncover the deeper story around the baby-care category, and what it found enabled the company to transform poor results into sparkling results.

When marketing drilled down and analyzed multiple points of intersection between products and buying habits, they found that buyers of baby products (essentially, new moms) might be buying the company's formula at a rate that represented low profitability for the retailer. But the same buyers purchased a number of the retailer's other products—like birth control pills, magazines and film—in the same stores where they bought its baby products. Seeing the formula category as a profit drain was calamitously superficial. Along with their baby formula, these consumers were buying a bundle of products that amounted to high profitability for the retailer. Smart companies rarely make a decision without benefit of a strategic customer management plan.

THE CUSTOMER ENGAGEMENT PROCESS

Proper perspective enables the championship salesperson to approach customers from a transformational position, focus his energy outward rather than inward and attribute to his role the value it merits. Playing catch with decision makers throughout the customer organization leads to insights about the customer's goals, needs and obstacles. This information is fed into the company, which has adopted a customer-centric, championship sales structure, and a strategic customer management plan is created. The Virtuous Knowledge Cycle positions the salesperson to deliver a directly relevant, tightly structured, fully aligned strategy to the customer. Now we move on to the final stage in the Performance Pyramid: planning and delivering that strategy.

10 QUESTIONS FOR REFLECTION: PREPARATION AND THE STRATEGIC CUSTOMER MANAGEMENT PLAN

- Do I proactively initiate games of catch and regularly meet with my customers to keep abreast of their evolving needs?

- Do I constantly feed information I learn about the customer back into my organization and orchestrate the appropriate resources against that knowledge?

- Do I regularly consider the efforts of my competitors and think about how I can distinguish my company's solutions?

- Is my organization structured so I can marshal resources to leverage what I've learned about the customer's needs and priorities?

- Do I understand who makes the decisions that affect my customer business and how these decisions are made?

- Do I seek areas of alignment between my value proposition and the customer's agenda?

- Do I devise customer plans based on assumption and conjecture? Or are my plans based on concrete knowledge derived from games of catch?

- Can I clearly articulate the customer's top objectives for the coming year? Can I do it in the customer's language?

- Does my team define a specific delivery plan for success?

- What are the potential barriers to a Virtuous Knowledge Cycle within my organization?

CHAPTER 9

Cresting the Performance Pyramid: Process and Presenting

It usually takes more than three weeks to prepare a good impromptu speech.

—Mark Twain

You have embraced a constructive mindset, harvested pivotal customer knowledge and applied that knowledge to a thorough strategic customer management plan. Now you and your championship sales organization stand poised to craft and deliver a specific plan of action to the customer. Atop the Performance Pyramid lies a seven-step process that lets you meet this goal.

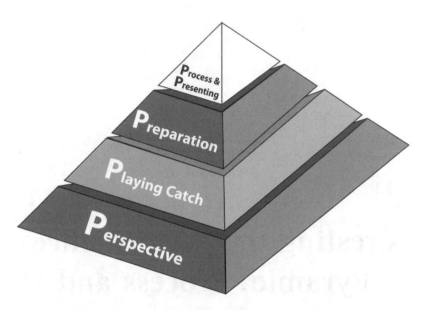

Figure 9.1: Performance Pyramid Featuring Process & Presenting

Like a rocket booster that sends a craft into orbit, the seven steps propel the customer relationship into a new sphere.

Though the customer engagement process begins before a call is made and ends after the call is over, it involves the customer at every point. Champion salespeople follow this tactical guide as a way to force discipline upon themselves. In today's breakneck corporate world, business leaders and decision makers are inundated at every turn, and those who can demonstrate a deep understanding of a customer's needs and eloquently articulate solutions will gain a vital competitive advantage.

1. Define and Align Plans

The championship salesperson's call planning begins with a clear understanding of his company's goals and priorities as they relate

Step 1 — Define and Align Plans

Step 2 — Engage the Customer

Step 3 — Identify and Confirm Needs

Step 4 — Present the Customer Solution

Step 5 — Confirm Mutual Commitments

Step 6 — Assess the Call

Step 7 — Execute the Agreed Plan

Figure 9.2: The Customer Engagement Process

to the customer. Development of a thorough strategic customer management plan reveals significant points of alignment between the sales organization's value proposition and the customer's needs. With these insights in hand, the salesperson and people in other functions begin to prepare a specific plan to address a particular customer need, a particular element of the customer relationship or particular requirements at a particular time. The strategic customer management plan provides the knowledge, areas of mutual focus and strategic insight; the customer engagement process provides a tactical plan for delivering the specific solution.

When you prepare for a date, you might conduct a strategic planning exercise, which reveals that the person you'll be taking out loves gourmet cooking but has a general dislike of jazz. The knowledge in the strategic plan will inform your tactical plan—in this case, you'll leverage one part of your value proposition (your ability to cook) but not another (your extensive collection of Miles Davis albums).

When you prepare to address a customer about your company's new product initiative, your first step is the strategic customer management plan, which exposes points of intersection between your company's product and your customer's objectives. When you undertake this task, you set yourself on a transformational rather than transactional course. You will enter the interaction thinking, "These are the ways in which our initiative fits your goals." You will not be thinking, "This is our new product. It's really amazing. Interested?"

The strategic customer management plan is a jumping-off point for crafting a specific presentation. Once you have identified particular points of alignment likely to resonate most powerfully with your customer, you need to decide how best to present your case. Here are five important guidelines championship salespeople and championship organizations follow when crafting the presentation of a specific customer solution.

i) Know your destination

Working backwards is sometimes the best way to put together an effective customer presentation. That is, determining where you want to finish can help you determine where you want to start. Your destination ought to be represented in a one-sentence message that encapsulates your entire presentation. For example, "Our product will accomplish the cost savings you desire" or, "Our expertise in this particular area will help create differentiation for you within the industry," or perhaps, "We can take this component of business out of your hands to let you focus on what you're best at."

Then, like an author writing a suspense novel when he already knows the ending, you create a storyboard to take you from A to Z. Forcing this discipline on yourself will help tremendously once you take center stage, especially in a customer environment that may be disarming. No matter your emotional state, you've got a clear map for yourself, and you know where you're headed. It is said of good social storytellers—the people at parties, for example, who always have small crowds engaged around them—that they always know why they are telling the story in the first place. Decide where you want to end up and you'll find it easier to get there.

Adjusting to the Customer Compass

Surprising your partner with two first-class tickets for an all-expenses-paid, week-long trip to Barbados is a great idea—unless, of course, she had her heart set on Hawaii. Put another way, if customers are thinking east, it doesn't matter how persuasively you lead them west. Before you develop a storyboard for the customer call, be sure the destination you're targeting acknowledges the customer's vision, not yours.

One salesperson we know—a champion performer who just happened to be a bit too keyed up on a particular day—went into a specific presentation excited about sharing his team's plan with the customer, a leading telecommunications firm. The salesperson was tremendously excited about the plan he and his team had put together. He took the customer through every detail of the proposal, carefully building toward the presentation's climax. After summarizing the final slide, he announced, "... and I guarantee this plan will deliver ten-percent growth over the next twenty-four months."

The customers looked at their pads, shifted in their seats and cleared their throats. After what seemed like an eternal silence, the senior customer executive looked up and said, "Ahem—that's a very impressive plan you've outlined. Unfortunately, we were thinking more along the lines of twenty-five percent."

ii) Make it a team effort, with team input

As the saying goes, two heads are better than one. The confluence of champion salesperson and sales-oriented organization—represented in the Virtuous Knowledge Cycle created by constant knowledge sharing among salesperson, company and customer—has especially positive implications for crafting presentations. With a company's resources aligned entirely toward the customer's goals, every person in the company—in sales, IT or finance—will have insight into how to deliver a certain message to the customer. In companies still bound by transactional thinking, the salesperson acts alone; since the organizational structure remains inward-facing, only the salesperson will have any insight regarding the customer's most pressing issues.

When a heavyweight prepares for a fight, his trainer, handlers and entourage instruct him on his opponent's habits, tendencies, history and current condition. He goes into the fight with a specific overall plan that includes room to improvise. If his trainers send him into the ring saying, "We actually don't know much about this guy—but good luck out there," he hardly has a fighting chance (so to speak). Customer interactions at a transformational level are conversations, not fights, but championship salespeople go into them as well prepared as heavyweight champions.

iii) Dig

Playing catch lets you know where the customer stands and what that customer wants to accomplish tomorrow. Building the strategic customer management plan helps you find points of convergence between customer objectives and your company's offerings. Now, go deeper—look for industry trends, historical patterns and external influences that might not seem obvious. Customers are invariably impressed when you show you've heard what they said; they're even more impressed when your organization demonstrates it has gone the extra mile.

iv) Don't equate presentation time to floor time

Transactional salespeople plan to fill their allotted presentation time with their own words. If they are given thirty minutes for a meeting, they plan a thirty-minute presentation. What happens? When questions and comments inevitably arise—a circumstance one should hope for—the presenters become more inwardly focused. They are intent on getting through all their material because they don't want the customer to miss a vital piece of information.

Championship salespeople do the opposite. They prepare a general presentation map, with key messages as the major signposts, and with backup material at hand. The main goal of the championship salesperson is not to communicate all this material; it is to encourage discussion. If you have thirty minutes, decide how much true "talking time" this represents. Be prepared to fill the half hour if required, but aspire to fill less than half; the rest should be occupied by productive dialogue.

v) Remember who the presentation is about

We know we've said it, but the principle bears repeating: remember to focus your message outward, not inward. A great presentation on a compelling topic can fall flat if it is self-oriented. This applies to even the smallest details. If, for example, your company, SuperCo, has learned that one of its customers, GiantOrg, needs to refine management of its supply chain, your presentation should not be titled *SuperCo's Expertise in Supply Chain Issues*, but rather, *GiantOrg's Supply Chain Goals*. Remember, the all-about-me syndrome is crippling. The ability to focus your presentation on the customer's objectives is golden.

Matching Presentation to Personality

Every company has a personality. Think about Nike's personality versus Prada's, Victoria's Secret versus Eddie Bauer, Ferrari versus Ford. Adapting your presentation to the personality of your customer can give it greater impact.

A presentation to the senior team at Starbucks, for example, is likely to look different than one aimed at the executives of Microsoft. Connecting with a customer's personality is a powerful tool—often as powerful as creating relevant messages and judicious solutions.

One senior executive put bells on his shoes for a Christmas presentation to a customer he knew liked to have fun. Another—a male executive accustomed to power suits and conservative ties—demonstrated his understanding of the transformative power of makeup to a cosmetics customer by undergoing a full makeover before delivering his presentation. Both were hits because both were informed by knowledge of what the customers would find agreeable.

The only caveat: rely on research, not assumptions, to determine the personalities of *those directly involved*.

Continued

A company's personality depends on its personnel, not necessarily the public's perception of it. The top brass at Starbucks might be a bunch of stuffy throwbacks; the steering committee for Microsoft might be starved for levity. There's only one way to find out: do your homework.

2. Engage the Customer

It's important to outline the context for your presentation. Like priming a wall for a paint job, anaesthetizing a patient for surgery or telling cottagers it's going to be a sunny weekend, establishing a strategic mental foothold prior to a call can help you build the customer's willingness and, potentially, enthusiasm, toward receiving your plan.

The process of engaging the customer occurs not in a single moment but over the course of days, weeks or months. A thorough pre-call begins the process. Setting the framework for success before you embark upon the actual call, meeting or presentation will allow you to focus on the delivery of your plan once you enter the room. The most important element of championship selling is that most fundamental of transformational principles: show the customer that you are on the same page. Transactional thinking suggests the salesperson should get the customer onside at the outset of the presentation; championship selling, based on transformational thinking, says do not wait until the presentation to get the customer onside. The work should be done beforehand.

With the agenda for the meeting in place, the overall presentation map complete and your key messages embedded, it's time to get the customer prepped. Your goal is to stoke the customer's excitement about what's to come. If a studio decided not to inform the public about the opening weekend of its forthcoming blockbuster, and instead just released the film quietly, a smattering of filmgoers might come across it accidentally. Through word of mouth, they might generate decent ticket sales. But the advertising campaigns typically associated with marquee films get people more keyed up than a cat playing with a ball of yarn. The studios tease just enough—saying generally what the film is about, who's in it and how it unfolds—so people go see the movie.

By sending a strategic pre-call communication to your customers, you achieve the same effect. You get them intrigued. Tell them generally what the presentation is about, who's going to deliver it and how it will unfold—but don't tip your hand. When the day of the meeting arrives, they'll be eager to hear more.

Sharing information in this manner also demonstrates to the customer how important you consider their needs, and it creates a deeper level of commitment on both sides. Substitutions or no-shows can dramatically lessen the effect of a meeting. Consider the absence of key decision makers, the extra time needed to relay the information shared, the broken-telephone syndrome that can serve to loosen the messages you have worked so hard to tailor. When you indicate how important the meeting is to you, you create a comparable level of importance in the customer's eyes, thereby minimizing the chance of non-attendance.

The more complex or sizeable the potential deal, the more critical it is to communicate with a customer ahead of time. Only a few salespeople apply this thinking. Everyone else loses tremendous amounts of revenue and creates built-in limitations to the client base. A pre-call need not relay detail; what it should do is briefly but definitively let the customer know a clear plan is in place, provide a general idea of how the plan will be communicated and state who will be there to present.

For example, here is a championship letter from a fictional salesperson, John Smith, to his customer, Chris, a vice president at a fictional company called Houseworks.

> *Dear Chris,*
>
> *I'm looking forward to our meeting scheduled for 1:30 p.m. on Tuesday, October 24 at your offices to share with you some of our thoughts on growth strategies for Houseworks over the next 18–24 months.*
>
> *Attending from our side will be Mike, Randy, Mary Taylor—an outstanding recent addition to the team—and, of course, me. I have included Mary's bio for your interest. Whenever time permits, please confirm that the participants from your team will include you, Pete Smith, Wayne Miller and Susan Devereaux.*
>
> *To ensure a productive meeting, we would like to propose the following objectives, agenda and expected outcomes.*
>
> ***OBJECTIVES***
>
> *1.   Prioritize top three sales goals for Houseworks for next 12–24 months*
>
> *2.   Refine market entry strategies for Magic Mop*

3. Determine 2–3 viable strategies for improving Magic Mop distribution by 25%

AGENDA

Table 9.1

Topic	Time	Leaders
Overall sales goals (prioritize three)	75 min.	John, Chris
Magic Mop market entry (fine-tune existing plan)	90 min.	Susan
Magic Mop distribution (brainstorm ideas to increase efficiency)	45 min.	Randy, Mary, Wayne

EXPECTED OUTCOMES

1. List of top three overall sales goals for Houseworks

2. Refined market entry strategy layout for Magic Mop

3. List of 2–3 distribution improvement strategies for Magic Mop

Please confirm whether this suits you, or feel free to suggest any modifications. Otherwise, see you next week.

Warmest regards,

John Smith

Presenting Even When You Aren't Presenting

Top champion salespeople plan every customer interaction as they would a formal presentation so they can maximize their effectiveness, learning and ability to deliver. Meeting a customer for lunch instead of in a boardroom equipped with an LCD projector doesn't mean you should be any less strategic or targeted in your approach. The questions you ask yourself before a formal presentation should be the questions you ask yourself before a telephone conversation, airplane chat or meeting over coffee: *What is my main objective for this conversation? How does it serve my customer's specific need? Given this context, what are the key messages I want to get across? What is the customer's likely reaction? What are the most effective ways I can respond?*

3. Identify and Confirm Needs

Your understanding of your customer's specific needs is based on extensive games of catch and thorough analysis of intersection points. Before you finalize the development of the customer solution, make sure you confirm known customer needs (so you can position the current solution with the most relevant information possible). And make sure you play new games of catch to uncover different needs that may lead to future business-building opportunities.

When customer needs—previous, current and fresh—have been properly grasped, use the combined knowledge to inform how you present the solution. Once the purpose and objective of the presentation are clearly established, you will be able to slip comfortably into explaining the proposed solution, confident of the needs you are seeking to address. Articulating the solution is the obvious core of any presentation, but first articulating the problem is crucial. Once you have placed your presentation in the context of a specific need outlined by the customer, you can communicate it with focus, relevance and power.

4. Present the Customer Solution

The pre-call has been executed, the message is ready, the organization is behind you, and you're ready to deliver the strategic plan. Championship salespeople understand the importance of investing time and effort to create a succinct, compelling, original message in a format tailored to the customer. Salespeople nearing the top of the Performance Pyramid reach its summit by learning how to become great presenters; they learn by blending concision with breadth, clarification with creativity, persuasion with substance, passion with restraint. They speak to customers with resonance and clarity; they encourage full championship potential on both sides.

In the old days, there were three simple steps in the ideal presentation:

1. Tell them what you're going to tell them.

2. Tell them.

3. Tell them what you've told them.

That was the transactional method. Your goal is to engage your customers in shared dialogue. The championship selling method uses a more collaborative view:

1. Tell them about your understanding of the situation.

2. Clarify and confirm that your understanding is accurate and current.

3. Based on this confirmed understanding, outline a solution.

The third step contains three sub-steps that inform every champion salesperson's delivery of customer solutions.

i) Open with purpose

Someone calls you on the phone, and initial hellos are exchanged. Then you expect a statement of purpose. If the person calling is your mother or best friend, perhaps this isn't necessary. But in most cases, you have a general curiosity about the caller's purpose. Once a purpose is established, you become more at ease. You feel more willing to engage because you understand your role, even if it is only that of listener.

When you begin a presentation or sales call, the customer wants to know why you think you're there, even if they think they already know. Even though you circulated a memo days earlier outlining the explicit strategy you wish to discuss, it's still up to you to establish your purpose. This is especially important when an additional person is brought along to the meeting; the new person has little idea what the meeting is about.

A solid, straightforward way to open with purpose is to briefly review the agenda circulated pre-call. When you give your attendees a final chance to make adjustments or add items, you demonstrate immediately that this is about their needs, not yours. And it's important to indicate how much time you plan to take—and don't go over that time.

Opening with purpose does not mean bursting into the room and launching into your presentation. It means being focused and forceful once you begin. Before you begin, there is time to establish rapport with the customer. This may involve exchanging pleasantries, or it may involve commiserating with a contact you've known for years about the fact that his daughter just went away to university. Building personal rapport is an important arrow in the champion salesperson's quiver. The pleasantry exchange shouldn't be allowed to drag on—it's ultimately up to you, not the customer, to get started.

When you open with purpose, you reiterate your objectives and you instill confidence in the customer by showing that you have mastery over and are keen about the material you will present. Conviction and enthusiasm are contagious, and the earlier you display both, the more likely you are to engage the customer.

Engaging customers on a personal level is as important as engaging them professionally. Rapport management begins the moment you enter the room; it continues throughout the call or presentation. Whether your relationship with a buyer is two weeks or twenty years old, you maintain constant awareness of fine cues and nonverbal signals so you can respond accordingly. You make subtle shifts in your behavior to match the mood or disposition of the people on the other side of the table. You recognize that people's lives are in constant flux: priorities change, strategies shift, crises arise. Championship salespeople never assume they will begin where the last meeting ended. They read every customer situation afresh, and try to respond in the manner most compatible with the customer.

The Importance of Not Giving All You've Got

English majors and aspiring writers invariably come up against a crushing irony. After they spend years expanding their vocabularies and learning to master complex linguistic structure, they are coldly advised by some teacher, editor or friend that a less verbose, more straightforward style would be more effective.

Transactionally minded salespeople often go into a call thinking it will be a failure if they don't get to show every one of their sixty slides in the Flash-introduced, effects-loaded presentation stored on their laptops. When you make the crucial transformation to championship selling you learn that a presentation is only a guide for playing catch with the customer.

Every aspect of your presentation must be disciplined—from clean slides (it boggles us how often we still hear people say, "I know you can't read the text on this slide, but let me explain it") to forgoing part of your talk in deference to productive conversation.

Research by Dr. Albert Mehrabian of UCLA indicates that approximately seven percent of a presentation's effect results from the words the presenter says, thirty-eight percent from the manner in which the words are delivered, and fifty-five percent from the effective use of non-verbal communication. When people actively engage in a presentation, they more easily process, and connect with, the messages it contains.

Championship salespeople never envision their message as the focal point; they see their messages as signposts between which people are encouraged to stop, chat and connect.

You can practice this. In any customer presentation, include only the information that has obvious and immediate value for the customer. Keep supplementary data on the back burner and have supporting facts at the ready, but don't be disappointed if they don't get used. If a poker player shows such a strong initial hand that the other players at the table concede the pot, he has no reason to show his cards. His time is better spent preparing his strategy for the next round.

Keeping Them Engaged

Even the best presenters can't prevent some degree of audience drift. One person is having trouble keeping his eyes open because he had to stay up for Letterman's Top Ten. Another is focused on eating her cranberry muffin. The pair in the corner have yet to wrap up a conversation that started in the hall.

Here are several tricks to seize and maintain audience attention.

- *Encourage notetaking.* If you attribute special significance to particular thoughts or phrases, you will keep people focused on your words. When you say, "I want you to write this down," or "Now I want you to remember this," you will get pens moving and eyes trained toward the front of the room.

- *Use all five senses.* Audiences are accustomed to seeing presenters' slides and hearing their words. Try to engage their other senses to keep them absorbed. For a breakfast meeting at your office, serve blueberry crepes or waffles with maple syrup. During a presentation, use interactive audiovisual aids or creative props the customer can hold and feel. (This encourages them to experience the solution directly.) If you haven't the time or resources for such efforts, use sensory words and images in your presentation to engage your audience.

- *Get them talking.* One of the most effective ways to get your audience thinking about your material is

Continued

by encouraging them to discuss it with one another. A request for audience questions is often met with silence because no one is bold enough to be first. But an exercise that requires audience members to talk with the person next to them about the section of material just presented turns participation active and forces them to process the material on a deeper level.

- *Single people out.* Remember how you'd ramp up your attention in that high school class with the teacher known for asking random questions of individual students? This tactic works. Ask periodic questions to prevent drift and to get everyone to maintain their attention. Ask a question of the group at large. Then maintain attentive silence as you slowly pan the room. A general rule of thumb is to count to ten before you speak again. In nearly every instance, the silence will prod somebody to speak up, kickstarting a discussion.

- *Share the lead.* If you occasionally hand over the responsibility of leading the discussion, you'll keep your audience's attention. Your aim is not to put people on the spot; it is to make them feel more significant. ("Jim, it would be great for us all to have some detailed background on your system. Do you want to get everyone up to speed?") Jim will appreciate the opportunity to showcase his expertise, and you demonstrate your willingness to step temporarily out of a leadership role to facilitate participation.

ii) Gain commitment

As a championship salesperson, you maintain a transformational view of the "close"—when you bring a dialogue to a successful point of convergence. (The transactional perspective views closing as a colder, more abrupt process that ends with slam-dunk statements like "Are you in or out?" or "Are we ready to do business?")

Gaining commitment no longer means sticking around until there is a signature on the dotted line. Instead it means building consensus around a particular strategy and slowly guiding the dialogue—sometimes over weeks, months or years—toward agreement on specific recommendations. Championship sales-people always lay out their proposed strategies in the customer's language, at the customer's pace, according to the customer's goals. They strike a delicate balance between urging the customer forward and allowing that customer the space to digest, consider and respond.

Eventually, the dialogue is intended to assume the form of an official contract or agreement. But the aim of the championship salesperson is to steer the conversation in such a way that agreement seems an inevitable conclusion rather than an inappropriate request. If you establish the purpose of the presentation, articulate the specific need to be addressed and direct a meaningful conversation, you ensure that you and the customer arrive at the same destination, at the same time, with the same vision.

As well, you need conviction and support to move the customer toward a decision even when both parties know it is in their best interests. Championship relationships are based on shared trust between salesperson and customer; both are pursuing a mutual good. Asking for the order is not an act of desperation but a necessary step in a broader, forward-moving process. In the purest form of championship selling, the salesperson need not ask for the business at all. When you execute the steps we have discussed—develop a championship perspective, play catch, prepare and present a customer-centric solution—you will have guided the dialogue in such a way that the customer will insist the proposed solution be implemented.

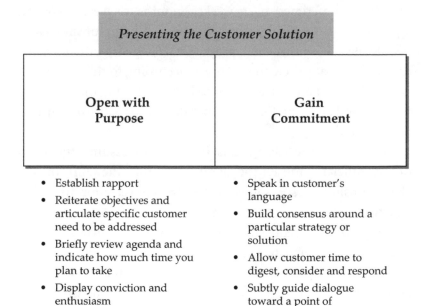

Figure 9.3: Anatomy of a Championship Presentation

What Should a Presentation Accomplish?

You've played catch with numerous decision makers throughout the customer organization. You fed the information to your company, which helped you assemble a great presentation. You delivered that presentation with aplomb, and you left time for abundant dialogue and useful feedback.

But you aren't sure you achieved your goals. Sure, the feedback was positive, but it was positive in a generic kind of way. There were lots of comments like "Good job," "Thanks for coming in today" and "That was great." The comments don't tell you a thing about whether the call was a success.

If you don't know whether you achieved your objectives, you probably don't know what those objectives were to begin with. It isn't always easy to determine if your presentation was a hit, but it's certainly easier when you have specific criteria to measure against. Part of any presentation should be a clear idea of what you want to get out of it. Here are three examples:

- *A good first impression.* The transactional outlook dictates that the purpose of the first interaction with a customer is to make a sale. Championship salespeople understand that the goal of a presentation is sometimes merely to establish a foothold for further dialogue.

- *Continuation of dialogue.* The purpose of the first presentation may be to create a context for the exchange of ideas between salesperson and customer;

Continued

the second, third and fourth presentations may serve to clarify that context and lay out specific points of alignment that have been generated by playing catch and generation of the strategic customer management plan. The number of presentations depends on the nature and complexity of the salesperson-customer relationship.

- *Purchase of a product or service.* In a high-functioning relationship between salesperson and customer, a relationship that is based on championship principles, the presentation to encourage or confirm a sale causes no awkwardness or unease, since both parties sense when the dialogue arrives at such a juncture.

The Most Common Pitfalls of Ineffective Presentations

Great presentations are memorable for many reasons. Poor presentations usually contain one or more of these five common flaws:

1. *Fear.* For most people, public speaking comfortably outranks death as the number-one phobia—so you're not alone if you experience sweaty palms, churning stomach and sudden brain lock when you stand before one customer or—yikes—an entire team. Your fear results mostly from ego or self-focus. Make a simple shift in thinking: this is about them and not you. You'll start to feel a lot calmer.

2. *Lengthiness.* Rarely do we see sales presentations that are too short; often we see presentations that are too long or contain too much information. In a sales presentation, less is almost always more.

3. *One-sidedness.* Productive presentations stimulate dialogue with the customer. The instinct to pitch always lurks near the surface and sometimes convinces us that the more we talk, the more we remain in control. In truth, it is when we get the customer talking that we exercise the most control. Fight the impulse to stay in transmission mode, and you'll see the difference.

4. *Lack of prep.* A high incidence of "Um," "Uh," or "Let me just double check that," excessive throat clearing or hand wringing, frequent glances at reference notes, vague or elusive answers to questions—all of these are symptoms of slack preparation. Nothing impresses an audience more than a presenter who knows his material cold. An apparent lack of mastery over the content can alienate the audience. There's nothing magical about the formula for preventing this: rehearse, rehearse, rehearse. Then rehearse one more time. Force yourself to stay in practice even when you aren't planning a specific presentation. World-class sprinters train year-round. Why? So that, when it comes time to deliver, they can slip into that zone without even having to think about it.

5. *Small-picture prep.* Many presenters feel they know their material inside and out because they've memorized every word, timed their verbal transitions between slides and taken care to include a sufficient amount of rehearsed

inflection. These are details. Details are not enough—
you must be able to explain the big picture. Champion
presenters do more than memorize every word, cadence
and slide. They understand how all the different elements
cohere into a single, definable message. In other words,
kudos to you for working your butt off to polish that forty-
five-minute talk for the prospective customer, but you'd
better also be able to capture it in ninety seconds. A big-
picture perspective also means being flexible in two ways:
first, staying aware of the customer's signals so you can
move the presentation along should it veer off the path,
and second, responding to new information or insights.
When their witnesses blurt something unexpected,
talented lawyers are able to adapt to the abrupt directional
shift without skipping a beat. Championship salespeople
maintain the same mental elasticity, always ready to accept
and integrate new information on the fly (though we
advise against hollering at the customer, *"A simple yes or no
will do!"*).

5. Confirm Mutual Commitments

Championship salespeople practice two important skills to
ensure accurate delivery of their commitments to the customer.
First, they clarify expectations before a room clears. Second, once
the room is empty, they make notes.

A presentation should always end with explicit clarification
of understanding, agreements, expectations and responsibilities
between salesperson and customer. When everyone knows what
to do, both sides leave with a general feeling of comfort and
accomplishment.

Once the presentation is over, the first thing a championship salesperson does is write down everything about the meeting, including outcomes, next steps and new insights. All this information will be used to deliver on commitments to the customer. Champions don't get in the car and pop in a favorite CD or rush home to catch a *Seinfeld* rerun. They capture every salient piece of information that resulted from the meeting. We have all made the fatal assumption that we'll remember that certain vital piece of information even after we stop for a bite, skim the newspaper or check in at home. Championship salespeople never allow such assumptions to divert them from capturing precise details of a meeting or conversation as soon as possible after it happens, then analyzing those details so they can be integrated into the strategic customer management plan.

6. Assess the Call

Every call, every meeting, every presentation, no matter how big or small, no matter how seemingly unimportant or inconsequential, can be used to improve your skills as a championship salesperson. This will happen only if you are willing to devote sufficient time to self-evaluation. No one improves without regularly turning the lens inward. By reflecting on specific tendencies, strengths and weaknesses over the course of several presentations, championship salespeople continually raise their own personal bars.

There is no better time for self-reflection than immediately following a customer call. The exercise of thinking about what worked well or what you might have done differently does not have to result in earth-shattering revelations to be worthwhile.

Self-analysis is valuable on two levels. On a personal level, the championship salesperson might identify propensity for moving around, distracting the customer from the messages he is trying to get across. On a professional level, self-reflection might help him realize he often spends too much time establishing positive rapport, thus having to rush through the presentation, diluting its effectiveness. If you recognize a tendency you can correct it, which can have an enormous effect on the overall impression you make.

Evaluation of the call or presentation does not stop at the level of self. It's important to assess what you've learned about the customer or buyer, what you've learned about the customer's organization, and what new synergies between your company and the customer might have surfaced in the course of discussion.

Jason, the senior vice president, is fired up. The Board of Directors, a heavy-hitting group, has asked him to make a presentation outlining the company's current situation and twenty-four-month plan, but they only have twenty minutes at the end of their monthly meeting next Thursday. He knows he had better pack as much into the presentation as possible.

Jason prepares thirty-four text-filled, legal-sized pages. It's important that he provide specific details of his plan so the Board will feel comfortable with it.

He enlists input from a colleague with a reputation for putting together powerful presentations. Ann's first piece of advice is to cut the presentation considerably— Jason is asking the Board members to digest too much in too little time.

Jason is upset. This is the person respected for solid presentations? And she's telling me to cut instead of to deliver as much as possible?

Ann asks Jason to do a dry run of his presentation. A few minutes in, Jason realizes that he sounds like a speed reader. After he races through the last few slides—he doesn't want any to go unseen—he quietly clears his throat.

"You didn't ask a single question," Ann says. "You never once turned the conversation to my side of the table. It was just a sprint to see whether you could get through the entire plan."

"It was that obvious?"

"It was that obvious." Ann lifts the thirty-four-page presentation deck and spikes it into the garbage pail. She's direct, thinks Jason. I like that.

"Tell me," says Ann, "in your own words, the most important few messages you want to get across to the board. Tell me as though we're just having a casual conversation about it over lunch."

When Jason is done, Ann says, "Now tell me at least two issues you'd like to elicit the Board's input on."

"Why?"

"Because it will give you a reason to ask questions."

"Why do I want to ask questions?"

"To get them involved instead of feeling they're just having a bunch of slides shoved down their throats."

Jason talks about some of the issues currently facing the company. Ann scribbles notes, then reads back the four key messages and two main issues of greatest importance to the Board. "Does that pretty much capture what you need to communicate to them?" she asks.

"It does."

*"You know inside that you're on top of your
business," Ann says, "but maybe you're feeling
nervous—unless you give the Board every shred of
evidence, they aren't going to feel the same way you
do. So you overcompensate by thinking the more you
go in with, the safer you'll be. In fact, the opposite is
true. The less you talk, the more opportunity you have
to understand what they're thinking—what they want."*

*Jason goes in the following Thursday, initiates
a rich twenty-minute conversation with the Board
members about the main pillars of his plan and the
potential issues facing it, and leaves stunned at how
enthusiastic and involved each and every person at the
table seemed to be—much more than when he usually
presents.*

I get it, *thinks Jason.*

7. Execute the Agreed Plan

If only one element distinguishes the championship salesperson,
it is the ability to execute. Execution is a simple concept, but
for many people it represents a daunting challenge. Flawless
execution requires attention to detail, high levels of cooperation,
continuous follow-up, an ability to manage the unexpected,
and, most significant, passion to deliver even when tremendous
hurdles stand in the way. The most direct path to credibility
with customers is consistent, unhindered execution of solutions.
Ordinary performers devise explanations about why things did
not go as planned. Championship salespeople find ways to make
things happen despite obstacles, and they are rewarded again and
again with steadfast customer loyalty.

On one hand, execution of an agreed solution represents the
culmination of the customer engagement process; on the other, it

represents only one phase in a long-term relationship maintained by championship principles.

The Follow-Up Imperative

You've had the experience: It's three a.m. when, out of the blue, into your mind pops a great joke, perfect sentiment or brilliant idea. In a half-stupor you tell yourself to scrawl it on the closest tissue or envelope, but an instant after that the rest of your brain persuades you to go back to sleep. You wake up for work a few hours later, vaguely recalling that you had a groundbreaking thought in the middle of the night. You struggle for a few minutes to remember it, to remember even the general context in an attempt to trigger memory, to trace the stream of associations that might have led to it—but the attempt proves fruitless.

The same principle applies in a customer presentation. Even the most junior decision makers today are required to juggle multiple ideas, suggestions and considerations, and no matter how compelling the information you've shared, effective follow-up is essential to ensuring that it sticks. Championship salespeople *always* follow up, for a simple reason. If they don't, things can too easily slip through the cracks; if they do, the person on the receiving end is prompted to action.

Less than half the things agreed to in a meeting get executed if there is no follow-up done by the salesperson. But effective follow-up turns into a to-do list for the customer and forces reflection on what was discussed, accomplished and agreed to. A particular senior executive we used to work with would come into meetings with our most recent follow-up letter as his current checklist for the project. That was all the proof we needed.

Follow-up can take various forms, but it should always be conducted in a strategic, relevant and—most important—timely manner. A few decades ago, a manager returning from a meeting might have two distractions on the way. Today's executive who just heard a knockout sales presentation, as she is returning to her desk, might chat with some colleagues about the direction of a separate project, duck into the company kitchen for a juice, stop to record a few thoughts about the initiative ready to launch in a few months—and so on.

Whatever form your follow-up takes, make sure it gets in front of each customer stakeholder or meeting attendee fast.

How fast is fast? This depends, of course, on your relationship with the customer, but a good rule of thumb is to conduct follow-up communication no more than two days after a call or presentation. Our usual practice is to leave a meeting, record outcomes, let the information sit for an hour, debrief with the team, and then—immediately—draft a follow-up letter.

If you have a great meeting, with plenty of agreements reached and next steps developed, and if none of it is captured formally, the meeting will mean little. How many meetings do you attend in a week? Can you remember the details of each one? Of course not. So after *your* meeting, you must a) get the details down and b) get them in front of the customer. As well, you need to follow up internally. The departmental resources of a championship organization should be poised for application once a call has been made.

Here is John Smith's championship follow-up letter to Don at Houseworks regarding the growth strategy discussion conducted two days earlier:

Dear Don,

Thank you for the time and energy you and your team provided earlier this week. The result was a highly productive meeting and even greater enthusiasm on our part to help Houseworks take its business to the next level within the coming 18–24 months.

The following outlines a review of plans and next steps agreed to at the meeting, including topic, owner and timing.

I will follow up with you within the next few days to ensure we have captured all of the pertinent information and to determine next steps in moving this agenda forward.

Best regards,

John Smith

Table 9.1

Topic	Next Steps	Owner(s)	Timing
Magic Mop market entry	Plan preliminary North American rollout of Magic Mop	John, Chris	By June 30
Magic Mop distribution	Finalize North American distribution channels	Susan	By July 31
Magic Mop competition	Initiate diagnostic to determine effective positioning levers for Magic Mop against competing products	Randy, Mary, Wayne	By July 31

Once you present to the customer and learn of the need for deeper financial projections, for example, you must be able to approach the Finance department and prepare swift follow-up analyses. Perhaps the customer wants to know more about promotional plans for the product it is considering carrying in its stores—in which case Marketing would need to collaborate with Sales to put the right information together in a timely fashion.

Internal follow-up ensures that everyone on the delivery team possesses an unequivocal understanding of his or her role going forward. This leads to optimum efficiency, uniform orientation, and unwavering confidence on the part of the customer.

So How Did We Do?

How do you figure out whether you've achieved your objectives? The best method is the one avoided by most people for fear of rejection: asking. Ask the customer whether the meeting met expectations. Ask what you might have done differently. Ask whether they would like to see more emphasis on any particular area. Championship salespeople do this because they still want to play catch. Their rightful attitude is that one never knows when the most pivotal nugget of information or insight is going to surface.

Most of us avoid inviting direct feedback for the simple reason that if we don't ask, we won't hear anything negative. However, if you ask for honest answers to relevant questions, you demonstrate to the customer that your primary focus is still on what they need. And which would you rather: a customer who feels you're sensitive to her needs, or one who never gives constructive feedback because she is never given the opportunity?

Following Up in the Electronic World

From job applications to negotiations of mega-mergers, business at all levels is conducted increasingly via the electronic superhighway. Electronic messages are very helpful for follow-up. Businesspeople delight in the ability to compose and fire off an instant e-mail in minutes as an alternative to writing, addressing, stamping and mailing a formal letter.

However, the speed afforded by e-mail should not be confused with a lack of potential impact. A precise, pertinent e-mail follow-up is as powerful as an ambiguous, irrelevant one is not. Championship selling has much to do with closing the sequence in a powerful way. Here are some guidelines:

- *An e-mail should be as professional as a letter.* Electronic correspondence dominates today's world and ought to be treated as professional correspondence. Pay attention to grammar, punctuation and structured thinking.

- *An e-mail should not replace a letter.* Though electronic notes should carry the same tone as professional letters, they should not be used as substitutes. An e-mail follow-up should be a few lines long—express gratitude to the customer for taking the time to have the meeting, for participating and contributing to mutual progress. Indicate that a detailed letter is on its way. (There's nothing wrong with attaching the letter to the e-mail, but mail a paper copy as well. E-mails are too easily lost, deleted, forwarded, ignored or Inbox-buried for eternity.)

- *A potential sender should be certain the customer welcomes e-mails before sending.* Before firing off *any* kind of e-mail—

follow-up or otherwise—it's important to find out whether your customer is e-mail-friendly. For every tech-savvy, BlackBerry-toting middle manager, there's an old-school CEO who considers e-mail a sign of the apocalypse.

• *An e-mail should not inadvertently undermine the relationship or the process.* A stand-alone e-mail follow-up to a discussion about a potential multimillion-dollar deal can unintentionally diminish the discussion's importance in the eyes of the receiver. A personalized, targeted letter demonstrates how important you consider both the customer relationship and this particular opportunity.

10 QUESTIONS FOR REFLECTION: THE CUSTOMER ENGAGEMENT PROCESS

• Do I a) play catch with the customer, b) use the information learned from playing catch to prepare a strategic customer management plan, then c) use the points of alignment revealed by the strategic customer management plan to devise a specific strategy?

• When I start to plan the course of a presentation, do I know my destination?

• Do I conduct thorough pre-call communication that outlines the expected participants, objectives, agenda and expected outcomes?

• Do I ensure a customer-centric tone to my presentations, right down to the title?

- Do I go into a presentation aiming to present every bit of information I have, or do I just let the dialogue evolve naturally based on key signposts?

- Am I aware of, and do I work to avoid, the most common pitfalls of ineffective presentations, such as lengthiness or lack of preparation?

- Do I record the outcomes of meetings and presentations right away to ensure I've got a clear, comprehensive record of agreements, expectations and next steps?

- Do I evaluate myself post-call, reflecting on where I struggled and analyzing areas for improvement?

- Do I follow up within two days of a meeting or presentation?

- Do I treat e-mail follow-up as professionally as formal letters?

CHAPTER 10

Seizing the Challenge

The world of business has changed. It has, in a sense, come full circle: today's most important skill is the most basic one of all, that of business building and customer development. Championship salespeople and their organizations share a firm understanding that sustainable growth and success in today's corporate world are driven by resolute customer-centricity. Those salespeople and companies devoted to the process of building customer value will not only triumph in the years ahead, they will determine the direction the rest of the market is destined to follow.

Organizations across the corporate spectrum have begun to shift toward stronger customer alignment. Leaders throughout the business landscape have begun to support the development of customer relationships based not on financial wizardry but on sales acumen. It is clear that the selling function is going to drive business success in the next decade and that those who sell are going to lead the charge.

We are at a true turning point, a watershed moment in the history of selling and the definition of business success. As a sales professional or leader of a sales organization, you stand squarely at the center of this junction facing an unprecedented opportunity. The complexity and competitiveness of today's business world makes the shift from transactional to transformational thinking critical. It is not enough simply to talk about championship principles; success means putting them into action. Here are six strategic imperatives for fostering championship selling—five that apply to championship salespeople and their organizations, plus one aimed specifically at academic institutions.

CHAMPIONSHIP IMPERATIVE #1: ENTRENCH THE CUSTOMER COMMITTEE

In most cases, the larger the company, the more committees one finds. Steering committees oversee the direction of strategic initiatives. Management committees ensure projects are proceeding according to the agreed-to critical path. Audit committees keep a closer eye on spending than a bear keeps on a salmon.

Such committees and sub-committees appear at every level of the organization, addressing every facet of its existence. Whether the governance board ensuring the placement and continuation of sound operating principles or the social committee brainstorming the theme for the upcoming Christmas party, all organizations, composed as they are of social creatures, love to encourage the formation of groups upon sub-groups to cover everything related to their businesses.

Everything, that is, except the most important thing. When was the last time you came across a customer advisory board, external relations committee or Keeping Our Finger on the Client's Pulse Task Force? Most businesses have a hard time operating without customers, so it stands to reason that a selection of their senior leaders should sit on a committee focused on their ongoing performance in that specific regard.

Who should sit on a customer committee? What kinds of things should it do? What should it talk about?

At the most fundamental level, the customer committee should be the storehouse of all critical information regarding a company's customers. Today, when Steve in Marketing needs to find out who his company's top five customers are according to revenue, he typically embarks upon a wild goose chase leading him to Lynn in Accounting, who refers him to Patrick in Communications, who passes off to Deepak in IT, who suggests talking to Danielle in Product Development. Eventually Steve cobbles the information together. The following week, when Terry in the Chicago office needs the same information, he takes the same circuitous route to get to Steve, now the holder of this vital list.

The customer committee would be the keeper of this information and more. What are each of those companies' objectives and strategies? How are they faring in delivering on those objectives? What are the shortfalls and what is being done to address them? How, if at all, is the company building upon or accelerating successful initiatives?

Broad information such as this, as well as granular information such as how much business was done with a given customer in a given year, would reside with the customer committee. Though others in the organization might possess some of the same information, everything learned or developed about a specific customer should flow into and out of the customer committee so that a centralized point of knowledge, documentation and direction always exists.

Who should sit on the customer committee? In most scenarios, the vice president of Sales, or other senior sales leader, is the logical choice to lead it. Other seats should be occupied by members of the Board of Directors and senior executives within the organization whose roles entail particular customer knowledge of one type or another. Aside from maintaining, organizing, updating and archiving information on the company's customers, this group would be responsible for efficiently relaying such information back to individuals or teams within the company when necessary. On a more strategic level, it would evaluate the effectiveness of the company's customer-related efforts, provide recommended shifts in direction, and, above all, ensure the organization remains unwaveringly customer-oriented in its approach.

CHAMPIONSHIP IMPERATIVE #2: NURTURE THE CUSTOMER RELATIONSHIP FROM THE TOP

We spent a good deal of space in earlier chapters discussing why it is of paramount importance for the sales function to be integrated at the top levels of an organization, and why neglect in this regard leaves a company fatally disconnected from its customers. Foremost among a company's top customer conduits is the CEO—or should be, at least. Too often, the CEO is considered an individual whose role transcends direct customer interaction. But, as we have stated, a true championship CEO not only makes a concerted effort to understand his customers, he places equal effort toward getting to know those who carry out day-to-day customer interactions on the organization's behalf.

To properly build and maintain the customer relationship, a championship CEO must adopt into his program more than the traditional arm's-length moves: occasional rounds of golf, client-celebration dinners and schmoozing at industry events or conferences. He must instead begin to see himself, and therefore encourage the rest of the organization to see him, as someone deeply versed in the customer's particular situation, someone as familiar with the customer's goals, plans and obstacles as those of his own company.

The only way to achieve this objective is through direct interaction at the highest levels of the customer organization. Customers do not want suppliers to guess at their circumstances; they want to feel understood. The championship CEO must make it clear that he wants to handle the most complex customer challenges. He must understand the tremendous value the customer can derive from his knowledge and expertise. He must undertake the effort to fully comprehend the customer's issues to either act upon them or suggest an alternate direction.

Establishing this kind of connection uniquely positions the championship CEO to spearhead the customer relationship from the top down. He feels perfectly comfortable, informed and articulate requesting partnership on a large strategic project. He is able to explain how the project will provide business value to both customer and supplier. He can advise the sales organization on what type of solution is likely to resonate with the customer rather than merely approve the budget.

On an equally important psychological level—some would argue more important—he is, simply, visible, neither the Wizard of Oz operating a network of gears behind a great curtain nor the dentist who comes in only after a hygienist has done all the work to pronounce it satisfactory. Instead, this CEO sets an example for the rest of the organization, while at the same time conveying to the customer just how important it is. For, if the CEO is paying that much attention, everyone else must be, too.

What can a CEO do to forge this connection? The same way any other sales leader would: by getting in front of the customer, asking questions and listening to the answers.

By connecting with the top levels of the customer organization, the CEO accomplishes a critical dual task. First, he gives himself the ability to tell those in his own company, with complete truth, I understand what the customer needs. Second, he allows his counterpart to say to those in his company, with utter faith, this supplier understands us.

CHAMPIONSHIP IMPERATIVE #3: FOSTER A MULTIFUNCTION FOCUS

A sales organization firing on all cylinders is a potent machine, and the individuals within it powerful agents of potential transformation. But, as we have outlined, the sales function on its own can only take an organization so far if other functions remain inwardly focused. Perhaps the most characteristic feature of any championship organization is its customer orientation across functions and throughout reporting levels. Customer-related information in such an organization flows easily among functions and is integrated effectively into solutions driven by sales leaders but facilitated by many others.

As a direct reflection of this multifunctional thinking, the championship salespeople in these companies naturally evolve into more than one-dimensional sellers. They become true customer general managers, guiding the customer in varied, sophisticated ways rather than merely trying to meet sales quotas.

To create a culture in which salespeople develop into customer general managers, championship organizations make different functions visible to one another and ensure their salespeople gain experience in each in order to speak to customers in a deeper, richer way. They broaden assignments in key functions such as Marketing, Finance and Operations to include salespeople, thereby broadening the skills they bring to the table when interacting with customers. The cross-functional knowledge developed by the championship salesperson has an exponential effect, since, with each bit of expertise acquired, this individual can penetrate new levels of the customer organization at multiple points and through multiple people.

The multifunctional mentality of a championship organization reflects back and forth between the level of the individual salesperson and that of the organization's overall structure. All functions, not just Sales, are aligned toward the customer and committed to understanding its needs.

CHAMPIONSHIP IMPERATIVE #4: CRAFT YOUR VALUE PROPOSITION FOR THE CUSTOMER

It may seem an obvious point to develop one's value proposition with the customer's goals in mind, but this principle is often overlooked. Organizations become overly focused on communicating their offering in a powerful way rather than communicating it in the context of the customer's needs and circumstances. Value itself can be defined as the product or service you provide and the way in which it is delivered—but a value *proposition* means something more. A proposition is a plan or proposal or scheme. The value proposition you bring to a customer must articulate not merely the words describing your service, but those words wrapped in a framework meaningful specifically to the customer. A championship value proposition therefore accomplishes three things. It describes your product or service; it describes the manner in which you deliver that product or service; and it describes *the reasons why that product or service, delivered in a particular manner, solves a problem for your customer.*

In developing a customer-centric value proposition, the championship salesperson, or championship organization, does more than arbitrarily select a problem facing the customer and then frame words to address it. Instead, effort is directed toward thinking creatively about the customer's entire business operation and developing targeted, explicit solutions to address underlying symptoms of significant problems. Often this means proposing bold solutions or innovative shifts; more often, it simply means digging a little deeper than your competition.

In either manner, the effort to address customer issues at their roots leads to value propositions that drive significant, long-term improvement.

Here's another way to think about it: Championship value propositions help customers better deliver on their own value propositions. No greater value is offered than the insight that enables the customer to serve its own customers more effectively.

Championship value propositions do not necessarily have to do with selling more products. They have to do with the various facets of a customer organization that influence selling.

Finding ways to help a customer reduce operating costs, for example, can be just as powerful as—and in the end, equivalent to—proposing to help it sell more crates of a certain product. Seek to understand how the customer receives and stocks merchandise. Determine whether there might be a more cost-effective way to manage orders, reduce unloading time at receiving docks or maintain inventory. The deeper a value proposition reaches, the more a customer will understand your desire to help it achieve greater levels of performance.

How do you find areas of true meaning for the customer? By espousing the principles outlined in this book—becoming and staying customer-centric, aligning all of the functions within your organization outward—and applying the practical techniques contained within the Performance Pyramid. Uncovering and developing consequential ideas is not complex. As with all championship concepts, it comes down to placing yourself in your customer's shoes—or, better yet, stepping directly into them by playing catch with senior leaders, taking the pulse of the organization at various levels and with various individuals, and seeking to understand what keeps key decision makers up at night. Championship salespeople marry dedication to the customer perspective with the skill to exploit the range of resources within their own organizations to generate ideas, validate conclusions and, finally, craft a value proposition that hits the right nerve at the right time.

The value proposition crafted according to championship principles works like the doctor striking your leg just below the knee with a rubber mallet, making it swing upward in reflex. The key to this trick is not the instrument used but the precise nerve struck. In other words, your product or service may be the right one, but a customer will respond positively only when you properly identify, and expertly strike, the right nerve.

CHAMPIONSHIP IMPERATIVE #5: FORMALIZE THE FUNCTION

In today's business world, the sales function has emerged as a prime differentiator. Those who carry out the sales function have become more vital liaisons between company and customer than at any point in history. In an increasingly complex and sophisticated marketplace, great products and services may still be the entry point, but championship salespeople are the difference makers.

In previous chapters, we have discussed the importance of formalizing training and development programs to cultivate the skills of aspiring sales champions and continue challenging the skills of those who have established themselves at championship levels. Organizations structured to identify and develop sales champions position themselves to make critical strides and develop a competitive advantage that becomes self-sustaining.

Formalization of the sales function in a championship organization happens in two ways. First, sales roles are defined clearly, developed systematically and evaluated according to specific metrics. Second, the individuals who carry out those roles are supported throughout the organization, whose functions are all aligned squarely toward the customer.

When a company takes the important step to formalize the sales function, it creates an invaluable side effect. Those aiming for, or solidifying, championship levels of performance feel emboldened. They request stretch assignments, pursue new opportunities to learn and grow, leverage others in the organization and solicit input from customers on a regular basis. This pattern validates the company's efforts to impose structure and discipline upon the function in the first place—which in turn reinforces the desires of aspiring champions to raise their games. The overall result is twofold: a sales function ticking seamlessly along and sales leaders delivering reliable championship service to customers.

CHAMPIONSHIP IMPERATIVE #6: GET INSTITUTIONALIZED

In a recent *BusinessWeek* article rating the top business schools worldwide, a prominent dean offers the following view: "[Business graduates] who are grounded in the fundamentals but who also have business-building skills are in high demand these days."

This statement, expressing the idea that both core and sales-type skills are desired in equal measure, reflects the increasing role of customer business development throughout industry today.

Where, in the past, it may have been felt that business building lay somewhere outside the fundamentals—that selling was an add-on skill—the notion gathering steam in today's corporate world is more accurate: business development—selling—is at the very core of a successful business skill set.

Recognizing the increasing importance of engaging, communicating with and delivering meaningful solutions to customers, and the resulting potential for top-line growth, business schools and other academic institutions are slowly beginning to focus their attention on customer business development training in addition to instruction in the traditionally "fundamental" general management skills.

The curriculum of Duke University, for example, includes a specific course, Managing Customer Value, whose orientation is distinctly outward:

> *Managing customer relationships goes beyond understanding your customers' needs and communicating with them. It is a business philosophy that encompasses all parts of the organization to provide a single integrated view of the customer, simultaneously increasing customer satisfaction and maximizing profits.*

Sitting before the business schools is a significant opportunity to make courses such as Managing Customer Value the rule rather than the exception. Our examination of the syllabus content of over 50 leading universities reveals that sales and customer development remains a growing blip on the radar screen of business schools, but a blip nonetheless.

Most often, such courses remain subsumed under the umbrella of marketing. Marketing to a consumer and selling to a customer are enormously different processes. One involves advertising copy, the other a live call. One requires gathering knowledge and studying purchasing trends, the other, asking questions and listening strategically to the answers. The former is a plan to deliver targeted, persuasive messages via creative media according to a specific timeline to get shoppers to stroll into stores or check out online catalogs, be drawn to certain products, and, eventually, come to feel they can't do without them; the latter is a series of rich conversations between individuals representing different functions and levels in which the attempt is made to learn about, and meet, the needs of the customer.

By beginning to devote more attention to customer development, business schools can send a powerful signal to the corporate world that they are marching in step with the increasing focus on, and need for, customer-oriented skills.

They will, at the same time, send a crucial message to their own graduates. By placing the selling function near the forefront of core business skills necessary to succeed, business schools can help reposition the understanding and definition of selling in the minds of aspiring corporate leaders. Current waves of business graduates, having had scarcely an introduction to true selling training during their school years, seldom emerge into the workforce trying to knock down doors for the best sales jobs. Even active recruiting efforts by successful sales organizations are often stymied, since potential recruits have often decided, long before being handed a diploma, that they do not want a job in sales.

Recently we were speaking with an executive member of the food and consumer products group preparing to speak with an assemblage of soon-to-be graduates from a variety of top universities. He lamented the fact that the profession of selling itself was a tough sell, since, for so many graduates, a job in sales was frowned upon. "We essentially go in fighting over the 290th-ranked recruit," he said, "since the 289 above him are targeting marketing, consulting or banking jobs. They don't even want to talk about sales." The irony is that these graduates ultimately end up doing that which they expressly intended to avoid: selling their ideas, knowledge and expertise to colleagues, clients and other investment houses.

The current scarcity of training in true selling skills makes it likely that even those carrying an inclination for sales into school will have had it unwittingly extinguished by the time they leave. At best, those fresh off a business degree might accept a sales role only in the hopes of using it as a springboard toward a more respectable role in marketing, people management or some other area.

One way for business schools to demonstrate their understanding of the importance of selling is to start adding concrete business-building tools to the more abstract, traditionally emphasized suite of management skills. Supplementing the ubiquitous case-study method, for example, the schools might begin to immerse students in customer simulations and role plays, drilling them in effective interaction processes and proper presentation skills. (Not to be confused with making a presentation to classmates. Preparing and delivering a presentation to a potential customer is altogether different than doing the same for a group of one's peers. If you disagree, try delivering a presentation to your own colleagues, then to a prospective customer, and see which one makes your heart pump faster.)

The same schools ought also to teach their students how to listen effectively, ask thought-provoking questions and manage complex business-to-business transactions. As we've outlined, top salespeople suppress the instinct to talk about themselves and instead ask skillful questions of the customer, listening to the answers with equal skill—yet where in academia do we find courses on listening to customer's needs? The answer is virtually nowhere.

This may be because selling, business building and customer development, though the oldest, most important skills in business, are challenging concepts—hard to explain, perhaps even harder to teach, and steeped in the ability to understand human complexity—whereas financial valuation, as an example, is comparatively straightforward. So perhaps the academic world has simply become accustomed to ignoring the fundamental principle of selling, inadvertently sending the clear message that companies ought to figure it out for themselves.

Beyond the ability to teach selling-specific skills such as those mentioned above, business schools have the opportunity to start molding new-world salespeople who think like customer general managers. As we have described in previous chapters, the championship salesperson of today is more than merely an effective communicator; she is a multi-skilled influencer who brings the breadth of all the company's functions to the task of crafting customer solutions. More than just an MBA graduate with a list of discrete management skills, she has synthesized these skills into the ability to understand the intricacies of a customer's decision-making process—and to respond with value.

Business leaders, sales leaders and academic leaders must create the agenda for change. So ask yourself: Where do I start?

You Mean I Have to *Sell*?

Prior to losing its auditing license in the wake of the Enron scandal in 2002, one of the top accounting firms in North America was cruising along providing auditing, tax and consulting services to leading corporations across industry.

While the company was still enjoying its halcyon period, executives conducted an informal survey of new recruits, asking what they imagined to be the number one skill required to ultimately make partner at the firm. The majority of recruits provided predictable answers involving strategic thinking and financial acumen.

The correct answer was, in fact, one that might surprise almost any wide-eyed business school graduate: the ability to develop new business, or to sell. The knack for fully understanding the company's services beyond simply knowing its product, the ability to articulate its offerings, the drive and precision needed to gain new clients—these were the primary skills being sought. This firm, like most companies, desired graduates who could do more than crunch numbers with lightning speed or perform eye-popping financial analyses. They wanted those who could look a prospective client in the eye and unwaveringly answer the question, "What service do you provide, and why do I need it?"

Later, when this answer was revealed to those already working at the firm, a second question was asked: If you knew coming into the company that selling would be the skill most valued by your superiors, would you still have joined? The answer, almost unanimously, was no.

An increase in the acknowledgement of sales at the academic level will carry with it a powerful consequence in the corporate domain. Having provided their students customer development tools alongside more conventional general management skills (finance, logistics, operations, marketing, human resources), business schools will produce more broadly skilled graduates whose value to their organizations will be significantly higher than the value of those ready to provide economic insights, perform whiz-bang diagnostics and hold their own in meetings with the corporate upper strata, but who, when sent to the front line to deal with actual customers, feel lost, awkward and, for the first time since entering business school, unarmed.

It may be said that the business schools, in order to ramp themselves up to a higher level, ought in fact to think back to the basics. They are, at the moment, stacked with courses teaching students how to count the beans and analyze them in different ways. The next step is for them to teach students how to acquire the beans not already present at the table. Most business school professors would agree that, if you don't have any beans, it doesn't matter how good you are at counting them—however, never having been taught the magnitude of, for example, selling skills, customer decision-making processes, strategic customer management or playing catch themselves, neither natural instinct nor conditioned intelligence move them to add such elements to their own programs. The peculiar result is that, as if preparing aspiring businessmen and businesswomen to run 95 percent of a marathon but not the final kick, their curriculums have covered everything up to the point of customer interaction, and then, suddenly, stopped.

By designing these curriculums to instruct students how to run the entire race, academic institutions, in addition to teaching fundamental business skills useful on the inside of organizational walls, will spur their graduates to think about the significance of customer interactions on the outside. In so doing, they will make the clear statement that becoming mountain movers in today's organizations means bridging an important gap by learning who your customers are, what they need and how to provide it.

No one in the corporate world today would dispute the importance of general management education in running a successful business. Business schools have done a remarkable job developing instruction in the quantitative, analytical and reasoning skills required to satisfy one side of the equation. Yet, to make a true, sustainable difference in the lives of customers, aspiring business leaders must also satisfy the flipside: the ability to sell, which, today more than at any point in business history, sets the ordinary apart from the extraordinary.

Triumphant sales stories dot the pages of history. Ancient examples include that of Marco Polo, who, by disseminating the silks, spices and other products he had brought back from China and the Far East, helped open the eyes of an entire continent to the world lying beyond it. In more recent years, Colonel Sanders, Ray Kroc, Michael Dell, Fred Smith and Howard Schultz have applied sales-based vision, persistence and commitment to building the global businesses Kentucky Fried Chicken, McDonald's, Dell, FedEx and Starbucks. Each of these companies came into existence through the ability of their founders to understand the precise desires of their potential customers, and each flourished on the shoulders of championship selling concepts and principles.

The success stories above, and myriad others, demonstrate that selling, in its highest form, can be a truly life-changing force rather than just a way to make a dollar. From these individuals we also learn that, even when the proper structure and circumstances are present, success requires effort, knowledge of one's value proposition, anticipation of requirements and a keen sensitivity for the inclinations of one's specific customers. Says Joe Pal, among the most successful insurance agents in North America, "Selling is really about educating people in value. You have to put yourself in their shoes. You have to win their trust. Once you've done that, they'll be willing to talk about the details of their unique situation. Once you understand that situation, you can present tailored options. I never recommend a program or agree to a customer request until I have a full understanding of that customer's circumstances. If someone comes in wanting to sign up for a million dollars' worth of insurance, I don't agree to it until I understand the specific needs that customer is bringing to the table. That way I can make sure I'm recommending a solution that's right for them. In the long run, nothing else counts for more."

In substantiating their curriculums, business schools can take note of the stories of Marco Polo, Ray Kroc, Joe Pal and all those in between. Whether their historic omission of sales has been intentional or unconscious, these institutions have before them a clear opportunity to help drive businesses to new heights. They serve as the guiding hand helping those with teeming ambition achieve professional focus. At the moment, that focus is like a lens with one tiny, but critical, spot obscured. It is imperative to cleanse this spot, revealing to those on the thresholds of their careers a choice whose legacy is long, whose promise is significant and whose practitioners are driving business transformation every day.

Index

Contact Us

Optimé International is a Sales Training and Development consultancy focused on developing high-performing sales organizations through Sales Championship™ real-life sales simulations, proven sales development processes and leadership development programs.

Optimé's clients include many leading Fortune 500 companies, and small and midsize businesses committed to maximizing revenues and sales talent potential.

You may reach Optimé International at the following locations:

Global Headquarters
4025 Yonge Street
Suite 135
Toronto, Ontario
Canada M2P 2E3
1-866-759-2053

United States Headquarters
Lakeview Tower
30021 Tomas Street, Suite 300
Rancho Santa Margarita,
California 92688
1-800-525-6418

Find us on the Web at www.optime.com

To fully experience the power of the Sales Championship™,
co-created by Optimé and Exper!ence it, Inc., please contact us at
www.saleschampionship.com.